The

COMMON CONTINENT
OF MEN

Kennikat Press
National University Publications
Series in Literary Criticism

General Editor
Eugene Goodheart
Professor of Literature, Massachusetts Institute of Technology

The
COMMON CONTINENT
OF MEN

Racial Equality in the Writings of Herman Melville

EDWARD S. GREJDA

National University Publications
KENNIKAT PRESS • 1974
Port Washington, N. Y • London

Library of Congress Catalog Card No. LC 74-80067
ISBN: 0-8046-9073-1

Manufactured in the United States of America

Published by
Kennikat Press Corp.
Port Washington, N.Y./London

Library of Congress Cataloging in Publication Data

Grejda, Edward S.
    The common continent of men.

    (National university publications. Series in the literary criticism)
    Bibliography: p.
    1. Melville, Herman, 1819-1891 - - Criticism and interpretation. 2. Race problems in literature.
I. Title.
PS2388.R3G7   813'.3   74-80067
ISBN 0-8046-9073-1

To Gail, Rick, and Steve
Without them, life would have been a "chartless voyage."

CONTENTS

ACKNOWLEDGMENTS

Given the focus of this study and the wish to illustrate my observations as fully as possible from Melville's writings, I have not represented adequately the views of others. Yet, for those views and for the facts and insights I received from their books and articles, I am grateful to the Melville scholars quoted in this volume. Less apparent but more meaningful is my debt to those persons who have touched this work in a personal way. No acknowledgment can fully express my gratitude to Robert L. Gale of the University of Pittsburgh for his unselfish help and especially for his sustained and sustaining interest in my work. For their generous assistance and encouragement, I wish to express my heartfelt thanks to Thomas E. Philbrick of the University of Pittsburgh and to Don Wilson of Clarion State College. Finally, I thank my students whose annual voyage on the *Pequod* has been for me a constant source of inspiration and instruction. To all of these, and to Herman Melville, I am deeply indebted.

The

COMMON CONTINENT
OF MEN

INTRODUCTION

Find out just what any people will quietly submit to and you have found out the exact measure of injustice and wrong which will be imposed upon them, and these will continue till they are resisted with either words or blow, or with both. The limits of tyrants are prescribed by the endurance of those whom they oppress.

Former slave and famed abolitionist orator Frederick Douglass spoke these words in his West India Emancipation Speech of 1857. In that same year Herman Melville, refusing to face further rejection by publishers and by the reading public, was virtually finished as a writer. Seven years earlier he had written to his father-in-law, "It is my earnest desire to write the sort of books which are said to 'fail.' "[1] That desire became a reality; except for a few poems and the unpublished manuscript of *Billy Budd,* he put away his pen and disappeared into the nondescript life of customs inspector and quiet retirement. Yet in those failures he left a striking dramatization of the oppressed-oppressor relationship echoed in Douglass's words.

By 1857 the slavery controversy had intensified to the point where the Civil War was inevitable. Melville's writing career, coinciding with the years of mounting tension (1846–1857), is a multifaceted mirror reflecting the multiple images of the being at the center of that controversy: the nonwhite. Adding dimension to the images is the intricate fabric of responses—fear, condescension, contempt, misconception, understanding and respect—that define a relationship between people of different cultures and races. The purpose of this

7

study is to look into the mirror of fiction and, by so doing, to clarify Melville's judgments, specifically his attitudes toward the dark-skinned races and toward interracial relationships.

In an age when American writers such as Bryant, Whittier, Thoreau, and Whitman spearheaded the attack on slavery, Melville was conspicuously silent. He played no part in the abolition movement. His letters and journals, the precious few not destroyed by his family, reveal nothing of his response to the dark-skinned races. That he should have remained insensitive to the plight of the blacks, especially during the race-conscious, strife-torn years preceding the Civil War, is inconceivable to readers familiar with his compassionate humanism, his frequent enunciation in fiction of the democratic ideals of brotherhood and equality. No one, however, has satisfactorily demonstrated whether Ishmael's "just spirit of equality"[2] embraced only the white, civilized man. Modern criticism is torn. William Sedgwick sees in Melville "an eternal feud . . . between the white and dark races."[3] Harry Levin has Melville ready to concede that "life is a blood feud."[4] Willard Thorp, on the other hand, claims that Melville was "unique among his contemporaries in his freedom from zeal and prejudice."[5] Milton Stern sees him as colorblind, noting that in Melville's fiction Polynesians and Europeans are "distinct faces of the same being."[6] The critical split, of which the above examples represent only a small sampling, has not been resolved by any detailed examination of Melville's racial attitudes.

For the most part, readers have sought clues to Melville's views on race in Benito Cereno, the story of black insurrection and atrocity aboard a slave ship. The result is more discord, some critics seeing Melville as antiblack, some as problack. Bruce Franklin, for example, calls the Negroes in Benito Cereno a "malignant destructive force"[7] embodying "savage terror and naked evil."[8] Charles Neider argues that Melville turns the Negroes into "poetic images of pure evil."[9] Newton Arvin sees the Negro leader Babo as "a Monster out of Gothic fiction."[10] Rosalie Feltenstein says that Melville "turns Babo into a manifestation of pure evil."[11] On the other side of the issue are those critics who read into *Benito Cereno* Melville's justification for slave rebellion.[12]

To the considerable bibliography on the Negro question in *Benito Cereno,* two comprehensive studies should be added. Charles Hampton Nilon in his 1952 University of Wisconsin dissertation—"Some Aspects of the Treatment of Negro Characters by Five Representative American Novelists: Cooper, Melville, Tourgee, Glasgow, Faulkner"—devotes a lengthy chapter to Melville and sees Melville's treatment of the Negro as an investigation of God's tolerance of evil and of the ambiguity of appearances. Sidney Kaplan in his 1959 Harvard dissertation—"Herman Melville and the American National Sin"—argues that Melville's attitude toward the Negro reflects the nation's mood from 1846 to 1856. Kaplan's brilliant study deals specifically with the Negro in bondage and places considerable emphasis on the historical framework of Melville's writing.

Aside from Nilon and Kaplan, few critics have attempted to examine the controversy of *Benito Cereno* in the light which Melville's other fiction affords; no study has fully explored what all of Melville's nonwhite characters may reveal of his conception of race. From *Typee* to *Billy Budd,* Melville's novels and tales, with few exceptions, display a variety of dark-skinned characters—Polynesians, Orientals, Indians, and Negroes. The plot and thematic function of these characters, their relationship with the white characters, Melville's or a fictive narrator's description of and editorial comments on them—all merge into a pattern suggesting that to Melville white and black, light and dark, are indistinguishable. One main thrust of this study, then, is to show that in Melville's fiction white men and dark, civilized and uncivilized, Christian and pagan, master and servant are, as Ishmael puts it, "federated along one keel," united on "the common continent of men" (VII, 149).

Yet the "common continent" is an ideal drastically at odds with another conviction that emerges from Melville's fiction. That conviction, a testimony to his honesty and his intense sense of justice, is that the oppressed, regardless of the nature of the oppression, are right to rebel. His militant position carries with it a searing indictment of the white man who has brutalized the nonwhite into an animal or tyrannized him into a fawning subservient—in short, denied the nonwhite his essential humanity. That denial is the basis of racial hostility and the tragic barrier to federation "along one keel." By refusing to see past his misconceptions, the white man sows the seeds of hatred. Invariably, hatred manifests itself in an oppressed-oppressor relationship, a conflict to be resolved only when the oppressed asserts his manhood and strikes back. Melville condones that rebellion. When the several races of the earth regard each other as men, not images, then those races are inseparably intertwined.

The pattern of Melville's response is neither overt nor entirely consistent. Generally, it suggests a growing social and cultural awareness, a movement from misconception to awakening consciousness to realistic judgment. In the midst of the composition of *Moby-Dick*, Melville wrote to Nathaniel Hawthorne: "Until I was twenty-five, I had no development at all. From my twenty-fifth year I date my life. Three weeks have scarcely passed, at any time between then and now, that I have not unfolded within myself."[13] Prior to his twenty-fifth year, he had shipped on a whaler, deserted ship, lived with cannibals in the Marquesas Islands, mutinied from an Australian whaler, beachcombed in Tahiti, served as harpooneer aboard another whale ship, sailed as a common seaman on the frigate *United States*. His discounting the crowded years spent in the exotic and barbarous outposts of civilization only serves to emphasize that his unfolding was a journey too, this one of the mind urgently probing the significance of all that the eyes had seen and read—and that "all" in Melville's case was extraordinary. Experience alone was inadequate; volumes of reading only spurred the thought processes. Experience understood, appropriated to one's self and made knowledge, is what he meant by that inner unfolding. The obsession to comprehend triggered the creative and intellectual growth. The recently discharged sailor of 1846 could bask in luxurious visions of the noble savage. The man who for ten years had "unfolded" within himself understood clearly "the primeval savageness which ever slumbers in human kind, civilized or uncivilized."[14] Accordingly, my general approach in the following pages will be to move chronologically through the Melville canon,[15] pointing out the awakening consciousness in individual works and emphasizing how the entire body of his fiction reflects a mind moving away from the convenient labels customarily attached to nonwhites to a recognition of the fundamental sameness of all human kind.

With a double focus charting the course—the duality of the nonwhite character and the white recognition of and response to that duality—a voyage through Melville's fiction will discover what direct autobiography has kept concealed, Herman Melville's estimate of the nonwhite members of the human family.

A TEXTUAL NOTE

At this writing the Northwestern-Newberry edition (N.-N. ed.) of *The Writings of Herman Melville* is in the course of publication. Thus far six volumes have been released: *Typee, Omoo, Mardi, Redburn, White-Jacket* and *Pierre*. My references to these works are to this edition. For the remainder of Melville's works, I have relied on the Russell and Russell reprint of the Constable edition, *The Works of Herman Melville*.

1.   *TYPEE*

When the inhabitants of some sequestered island first descry the "big canoe" of the European rolling through the blue waters towards their shores, they rush down to the beach in crowds, and with open arms stand ready to embrace the strangers. Fatal embrace! They fold to their bosoms the vipers whose sting is destined to poison all their joys; and the instinctive feeling of love within their breasts is soon converted into the bitterest hate.

On January 3, 1841, at the age of twenty-two, Herman Melville shipped as a common seaman on the *Acushnet* of Fairhaven, a whaler sailing from New Bedford. Eighteen months later the vessel lay at anchor in the harbor of Nuku-heva. Chafing at the dull routine and harsh conditions of shipboard life, lured by the lush green of an island paradise, Melville, along with companion Toby Green, deserted. Thus began an adventure that would yield raw material for his first response in fiction to a nonwhite race and culture. These nonwhites were the natives of the Marquesas Islands, among the most primitive of the Polynesians. Melville's observations of them—their appearance, their character, their relative merits and defects in comparison to the white man—form the bulk of his first published work, *Typee: A Peep at Polynesian Life.*

Part romance, part travel book, *Typee* eludes classification; the distinction between fiction and autobiography is blurred. As might be expected, point of view poses a problem. Melville creates a narrator, Tommo, a green sailor on a land-sick ship longing for the exotic shore. In his desertion from the ship and harrowing flight into the island's interior, his hairbreadth escape from hostile savages, Tommo is cast as romantic hero.

13

In what will become a customary artistic weakness, however, Melville constantly blends the voice of the subjective narrator with that of the travel-book writer and propagandist. Whatever the voice, the tone—the attitude—is consistently that of Herman Melville, twenty-five years old, looking back on and emotionally probing the implications of an actual experience. Detachment, be it a sin or a virtue, was not Melville's forte; rarely could he achieve that vantage point above and apart from the passionate experiences that marked his early life. As Jay Leyda observes, "There is a link between Melville's experiences and his works, which are all a transmutation, to some degree, of a reality he had observed or lived."[1] Raymond Weaver refuses to separate Melville from his narrators: "The overwhelming bulk of Melville's writing is self-expression and satire; the hero is always himself, either in his own undisguised person or else thinly masked in all sorts of romantic and allegorical finery."[2] In the case of *Typee,* Tommo is Melville's guise and, for the sake of consistency, will be treated as such in this and the next chapter. Regardless of point of view, beneath the convenient labels of romance, travel book, and autobiography lies the story of a mind groping to define a relationship with other beings. As Milton R. Stern aptly puts it, *Typee* is "the story of a man's discovery of his relationship to the world."[3] Implicit in that discovery is his awakening to the conditions from which interracial harmony and hostility spring.

What immediately strikes the reader of *Typee* is Tommo's first response to the physical qualities of the natives. No doubt, confinement in a floating hovel would add considerable luster to a young man's vision of beauty, but Tommo's admiration is tinged with genuine surprise. The "strangely jumbled anticipations" that haunted him during the passage to the Marquesas—"strange visions of outlandish things . . . cannibal banquets . . . tatooed chiefs . . . sunny valleys planted with bread-fruit trees . . . savage woodlands guarded by horrible idols . . ."[4]—apparently did not include anything beautifully human. When the Polynesian girls, or "mermaids," board the anchored vessel, he exclaims: "Their appearance perfectly amazed me; their extreme youth, the light clear brown of their complexions, their delicate features, and inexpressibly graceful figures, their softly moulded limbs, and free unstudied action, seemed as strange as beautiful" (p. 15). Tommo repeatedly returns to their beauty, and his initial "amazed" response is emphatically confirmed. No longer a green sailor gaining his first excited glimpse of South Sea "mermaids," but a man speaking from the point of view of one who has lived with the natives and observed them carefully, Tommo writes: "In beauty of form they surpassed anything I had ever seen. Not a single instance of natural deformity was observable. . . . Every individual appeared free from those blemishes which sometimes mar the effect of an otherwise perfect form. But their physical excellence did not merely consist in an exemption from these evils; nearly every individual of their number might have been taken for a sculptor's model" (p. 180). The attitude here is one of uninhibited admiration of physical perfection. Significantly, these "sculptor's model[s]" are "light olive," sometimes "darker," "golden," or of a "more swarthy hue" (p. 183). To Tommo physical beauty was not the exclusive property of the white skin. As Harry Levin has observed, ". . . Melville is esthetically entranced by the passionate dances of the Polynesians, and his racial consciousness begins to undergo a radical transposition when he envisions them as pieces of 'dusky statuary.' "[5]

The individuals described in *Typee* are, like the group portraits cited above, magnificent physical specimens. The aspect of the chieftain Mehevi is "imposing," and "from the excellence of his physical proportions, [he] might certainly have been regarded as one of Nature's noblemen" (p. 78). Not even age mars physical attractiveness. One patriarch of "gigantic frame," though bowed by age, "retained all . . . [his] original magnitude and grandeur of appearance" (p. 29). Old Marheyo, Tommo's adopted father in the valley, is another "native of gigantic frame" (p. 83). Young warriors are equally imposing. Tommo's guardian Kory-Kory is "about six feet in height, robust, and well made" (p. 83). Describing young Marnoo, an island wanderer, Tommo again employs an art image to express the "matchless symmetry of his form":

His unclad limbs were beautifully formed; whilst the elegant outline of his figure, together with his beardless cheeks, might have entitled him to the distinction of standing for the statue of the Polynesian Apollo; and indeed the oval of his countenance and the regularity of every feature reminded me of an antique bust. But the marble repose of art was supplied by a warmth and liveliness of expression only to be seen in the South Sea Islands under the most favorable developments of nature. The hair of Marnoo was a rich curling brown, and twined about his temples and neck in little close curling ringlets, which danced up and down continually when he was animated in conversation. [Pp. 135–36]

It is interesting to note that Melville's prime example of physical attractiveness, Billy Budd, is described some four decades later in terms echoing those employed in the above account of Marnoo. Budd, too, is an "Apollo";[6] Budd, too, has a face that seems the work of a "Greek sculptor."[7] The similarity suggests that, so far as Melville was concerned, neither the brown skin nor the white skin was a vital factor in the composition of what Walt Whitman called the "human form divine."

Lavish as his descriptions of the Polynesians may be, Tommo's admiration soars when he draws the portrait of Fayaway, the "very perfection of female grace and beauty" (p. 85). The "extraordinary beauty" of Fayaway's form and countenance dominates Tommo's account of his experience in the Typee Valley, as evidenced by his repeated—and, by his own admission, inadequate—attempts to recreate for the reader this embodiment of feminine loveliness. Throughout his narrative Tommo embellishes nearly every reference to Fayaway with some worshipping comment on her physical aspect. The result is that, though she emerges but dimly as a character, she remains in the reader's mind—and certainly in Tommo's—as the ultimate splendor of the paradisiacal valley. Fayaway's face is "a rounded oval, . . . each feature as perfectly formed as the heart or imagination of man could desire." It is a "countenance, singularly expressive of intelligence and humanity." Her lips are full and, when parted, disclose "teeth of dazzling whiteness." Her mouth is "rosy," her hair of "deepest brown, parted irregularly in the middle" and flowing "in natural ringlets over her shoulders" and, at times, covering "her lovely bosom." Her "strange blue eyes" are "like stars," her hands "as soft and delicate as those of any countess," her feet "as diminutive and fairly shaped as those which peep from beneath the skirts of a Lima lady's dress." Fayaway's color is no small contribution to her beauty: "Her complexion was a rich and mantling olive, and when watching the glow upon her cheeks . . . [Tommo] could almost swear that beneath the transparent medium there lurked the blushes of a faint vermilion" (p. 85). At no time in his narrative does skin color detract from Fayaway's beauty; in fact, her olive hue complements her figure, which Tommo would match "against any beauty in the world."

Undoubtedly, Tommo's worship of Fayaway's seductive beauty is grounded in a romantic bias: he is a "declared admirer." Her description, however, applies "to nearly all the youthful portion of her sex in the valley. Judge ye then, reader, what beautiful creatures they must have been" (p. 87). In describing these "creatures," Tommo again employs a classical reference: they are "a band of olive-coloured Sylphides on the point of taking wing" (p. 152). The fullest tribute to these olive-hued nymphs he pays at the expense of white femininity:

I should like to have seen a gallery of coronation beauties, at Westminster Abbey, confronted for a moment by this band of Island girls; their stiffness, formality, and affectation contrasted with the artless vivacity and unconcealed natural graces of these savage maidens. It would be the Venus de' Medici placed beside a milliner's doll. [P. 161]

Readily discernible in Tommo's scornful attitude in the foregoing passage is the conventional romantic admiration of the noble savage unmarred by the artificial embellishments of civilization; however, as William Sedgwick argues, "True as this may be, it is not the whole truth. . . . If there is literary convention here there is the pressure of personal responses to animate it."[8] Sedgwick continues, "It appears more and more that the picture painted of Typee Valley was not at last view an adoption and adaptation to himself of an external literary ideal. It has far too much warmth and flowing fulness. . . . It came from within, out of personal recollections."[9] And Stern concurs, saying, ". . . By no means is his agreement [with Rousseauism] a back to nature movement, transcendental or otherwise."[10] In any event, the reader cannot ignore the "matchless symmetry of form" and feature which appeals to the appreciative observer that Tommo shows himself to be in this work. No mere romancer depicting the savage exclusively through the literary eyeglasses of other writers, he is, as Charles Anderson puts it, "a sight-seer, with a professional's eye for beauty."[11] He repeatedly insists that he is presenting an accurate portrait, "no fancy sketch" but a picture "drawn from the most vivid recollections" (p. 86).

Similar to the Venus–milliner's doll contrast is Tommo's estimate of the white physique compared to the brown. At a tribal festival he observes:

. . . I could not avoid comparing them with the fine gentlemen and dandies who promenade such unexceptionable figures in our frequented thoroughfares. Stripped of the cunning artifices of the tailor, and standing forth in the garb of Eden—what a sorry set of round-shouldered, spindle-shanked, crane-necked varlets would civilized men appear! Stuffed calves, padded breasts, and scientifically cut pantaloons would avail them nothing, and the effect would be truly deplorable. [Pp. 180–81]

Granted, the essential terms of the contrast are civilized, artificial man versus primitive, natural man; but, throughout the narrative, primitive and natural are linked with the nonwhite skin. In essence, whenever Tommo compares the white form with the olive, the latter emerges in a decidedly more attractive light.

Tommo's account of the natures of the brown-skinned Apollos and Venuses adds an admirable dimension to their physical portraits: though never exposed to Scripture or to pulpit accounts of the example of Christ, they are often Christian in spirit and in their relations with their fellows. Tommo cannot accept the horrible reputations attributed to these "innocent people." In fact, he finds an ideal social state. "No one appeared to assume any arrogant pretensions. There was little more than a slight difference in costume to distinguish the chiefs from the other natives. All appeared to mix together freely" (p. 185). What little labor they perform is done in a spirit of helpfulness and equality, several, for example, joining in "good cheer" to move a stone that might be carried by two. "Every action of life" is done "in concert and good fellowship" (p. 203). The fishing expeditions, the results of which are equally distributed to all the inhabitants of the valley, the tapa manufacturing, the gathering of fruit— all these activities are performed in harmony and without the exhortations of an overseer. In short, "Everything went on in the valley with a . . . smoothness unparalleled . . . in the most select, refined, and pious associations of mortals in Christendom" (p. 200). Tommo attributes this harmonious social order to "an inherent principle of honesty and charity towards each other," to the "indwelling . . . universally diffused perception of what is *just* and *noble*" (p. 201). Among the natives there are no thefts, no threats of assassination, no covetousness, no quarrels, no selfishness, no dishonesty, no lack of charity. Tommo's response to their natures, like his reaction to their physical appearance is one of amazement: "They deal more kindly with each other, and are more humane, than many who study essays on virtue and benevolence, and who repeat every night that beautiful prayer breathed first by the lips of the divine and gentle Jesus" (p. 203). As if in response to the "divine and gentle Jesus," they are bound to one another by "strong affection." "The love of kindred I did not so much perceive, for it seemed blended in the general love; and . . . all were treated as brothers and sisters" (p. 204).

As previously suggested, the innocence and humanity of

these nonwhites can be accounted for—in part—by their not
having been offered the questionable gift of knowledge and
by their fusion with a natural element untouched by the
corrupting hands of civilization. Accordingly, skin color may
not be a determining factor in their Christian natures. What
must be acknowledged, however, is that, until his final days in
the Typee Valley, Tommo does not associate the dark skin
with animal instincts; nor is the nature within that dark skin
morally and ethically inferior to the nature of the white man.
In fact, he invests the natives with a character that shines
brightly beside the shadowy character of white civilization:
"I will frankly declare that after passing a few weeks in this
valley of the Marquesas, I formed a higher estimate of human nature than I had ever before entertained. But alas! since
then I have been one of the crew of a man-of-war, and the
pent up wickedness of five hundred men has nearly over-
turned all my previous theories" (p. 203).

Just as he insists on the accuracy of his sketches of the
physical beauty of the Polynesians, Tommo emphasizes the
fidelity of his account of their character. After describing
the bond of affection that unites these people, he asserts, "Let
it not be supposed that I have overdrawn this picture. I have
not done so" (p. 204). Newton Arvin is representative of a
host of scholars who accept the genuineness of Melville's
comments: "In Melville's picture of the tranquility that mostly
reigned in the valley, there is nothing that cannot be confirmed."[12] Lewis Mumford agrees, arguing that Melville
avoided "sentimental gloss": "If Melville had trusted his eyes
less and his wits more he might perhaps have disclosed facts
which were sealed to him: he might also have muddled and
misinterpreted everything. The very limitations of Melville's
descriptions give one confidence in their authenticity."[13]

If any facet of Tommo's account is "overdrawn," his sinister portrait of the natives in the last four chapters of *Typee*
would seem to be the one. As has been demonstrated, the
overwhelming emphasis in *Typee* is on the attractiveness and
the kindly natures of the natives. In chapter 31, however,
the portrait turns sinister. In a darkened hut, firelight eerily
flickers on the "savage lineaments" of a "wild-looking group,"

a circle of "evil beings in the act of working a frightful in-
cantation." Faces previously associated with Greek divinity
become hideous with suggestions of the bestial. A native
returning with a war party has "inflamed eyes [that] rolled
in their sockets." A chieftain is described in an equally savage
light: "His cheek had been pierced by the point of a spear,
and the wound imparted a still more frightful expression to
his hideously tattooed face." Natives, who earlier never quar-
reled, are in the final chapter embroiled in an argument during which "blows were struck, wounds were given, and blood
flowed." In dramatic contrast, the natives suddenly become
savages whose appearance and actions fill Tommo with "fore-
bodings of evil," and he determines to leave the valley. In the
thrilling escape chapters of *Typee,* then, Tommo appears
to negate the bulk of his favorable testimony in behalf of the
Polynesians, and, in so doing, to suggest that beneath the
brown skin lurks an evil heart. As Sedgwick states the problem, ". . . We cannot help feeling that the narrative climax is
deeply at odds with a great part of the book. . . . For the
natives of Typee, as Melville has described them at length, are
hardly the kind of people from whom a man would have to
fly for his life, or, for that matter, a man would care to take
leave of under any circumstances whatever."[14] Confronted
with the conflicting portrait composed of idyllic virtue and
savage evil, of beauty and ugliness, the reader must conclude
that Tommo's response to the Polynesians is either contradic-
tory or ambivalent.

Perhaps the conflict lies not so much in mixed attitude as
in the problems posed by the type of work that *Typee* is—
romance. The inhabitants of paradise turn savage when Melville requires a dramatic close for a work that had begun as
a romance but had become a plotless, suspenseless travel
book. The early chapters are not lacking in those qualities
which create interest in the romance. Action and suspense
are there. Will Tommo and his companion, Toby, escape
from the whaler? What dangers will they meet in the interior
of the island? Will they find food and shelter? Are the natives

they meet the friendly Happars or the cannibalistic Typees? Will Toby escape and bring help? And most dreadful of all, is Tommo to be the main course at a Typee feast? The adventure tale is off to a thrilling beginning. The questions, however, are resolved early, leaving the narrator the leisurely task of providing his civilized readers with a "Peep at Polynesian Life." "Peep" is understating the case. Chapters 14 to 31 are devoted to a multitude of observations—about everything from the contents of a housewife's cupboard to the craft of making tapa. The information, as such, is interesting but hardly the stuff from which a successful yarn is spun. An antagonist must be provided; danger should be close at hand; the hero should be more than a curious observer. As Leon Howard has noted, Tommo "could hardly have afforded to give the impression that his real fears were really unfounded or have allowed his readers to close the book without being relieved of the suspense in which the hints of cannibalism had held them. . . ."[15]

Thus, when the "peep" is concluded, Tommo relates two events that return the narrative to the realm of romantic adventure. He discovers that the natives are determined to tattoo him, and he discovers evidence of cannibalism. His initial reactions of horror are followed by a bitter awareness of isolation: "There was no one with whom I could freely converse; no one to whom I could communicate my thoughts; no one who could sympathize with my sufferings" (p. 231). The innocent Apollos become sinister antagonists. Action and suspense are again the focal points, highlighted by the escape and rescue climax. Anderson remarks that "the whole scene of the rescue itself is romantic and unconvincing, apparently written in haste and . . . with a view to making himself [Melville] a hero."[16] If, as is probable in the concluding chapters, Melville is fictionally enhancing actual experience, the olive-skinned wonders are associated with evil because the author requires an exciting climax for his book.

Native savagery may satisfy the exigencies of romantic fiction, but that savagery is not necessarily "deeply at odds" with the positive portrait Tommo has drawn. Indirectly, and perhaps unconsciously, he has prepared the reader for the dichotomy of character, abrupt as the shift may appear. His revelation of the dark side of Polynesian nature reflects his complex response to the white man's relationship with an alien, dark-skinned, primitive people. From the outset of his experience, he is aware of the white man's ignorance of the Polynesian world:

Within the last few years American and English vessels engaged in the extensive whale fisheries of the Pacific have occasionally, when short of provisions, put into the commodious harbor which there is in one of the islands; but a fear of the natives, founded on a recollection of the dreadful fate which many white men have received at their hands, has deterred their crews from intermixing with the population sufficiently to gain any insight into their peculiar customs and manners. [P. 6]

Whatever labels one may attach to *Typee,* it is an account of Tommo's intermixing with the natives and acquiring that "insight." With it comes the recognition of the white man's devastating impact on Polynesian life. In Tommo's narrative the whites emerge as physically inferior, rapacious, polluting forms of life; above all, they are responsible for Polynesian savagery: "It may be asserted without fear of contradiction, that in all cases of outrages committed by Polynesians, Europeans have at some time or other been the aggressors, and that the cruel and bloodthirsty disposition of some of the islanders is mainly to be ascribed to the influence of such examples" (p. 27).

Tommo associates the white civilized man with diseases polluting the lives of the Polynesians. From an 1846 vantage point that included a brief residence in Hawaii, he claims, the "once smiling" Hawaiians are "now diseased, starving, and dying" (p. 124). They use the native drink "arva" not as "a minister to social engagement" (as was the case before the coming of the whites) but as a treatment "in combating the ravages of [venereal] disease for whose frightful inroads the ill-starved inhabitants of that group [the Hawaiian Islands]

are indebted to their foreign benefactors" (p. 165). No
sooner does conversion occur than "disease, vice, and premature death make their appearance" (p. 195). Tommo's
indictment below speaks for itself and summarizes accurately his attitude throughout *Typee* toward, not the civilized
man per se, but the *white* man: "Thrice happy are they who,
inhabiting some yet undiscovered island in the midst of the
ocean, have never been brought into contaminating contact
with the white man" (p. 15).

The white man not only contaminates; by "signal infrac-
tion[s] of the rights of humanity" (p. 17), he provokes the
Polynesian into savagery. Repeatedly Tommo questions what
people deserve the term "savages." The following passage,
representative of his reflections on European cruelties, deserves quoting in full:

> The enormities perpetrated in the South Seas upon some of the
> inoffensive islanders wellnigh pass belief. These things are seldom
> proclaimed at home; they happen at the very ends of the earth;
> they are done in a corner, and there are none to reveal them. But
> there is, nevertheless, many a petty trader that has navigated the
> Pacific whose course from island to island might be traced by a
> series of cold-blooded robberies, kidnappings, and murders, the
> inquity of which might be considered almost sufficient to sink her
> guilty timbers to the bottom of the sea.
>
> Sometimes vague accounts of such things reach our firesides,
> and we coolly censure them as wrong, impolitic, needlessly severe,
> and dangerous to the crews of other vessels. How different is our
> tone when we read the highly-wrought description of the massacre
> of the crew of the Hobomak by the Feejees; how we sympathise
> for the unhappy victims, and with what horror do we regard the
> diabolical heathens, who, after all, have but avenged the unpro-
> voked injuries which they have received. We breathe nothing but
> vengeance, and equip armed vessels to traverse thousands of miles
> of ocean in order to execute summary punishment upon the
> offenders. On arriving at their destination, they burn, slaughter,
> and destroy, according to the tenor of written instructions, and
> sailing away from the scene of devastation, call upon all Christen-
> dom to applaud their courage and their justice. [Pp. 26–27]

Tommo's denunciation of the barbarity and "remorseless
cruelty" of the beings who appropriately deserve the title of
"savage" climaxes in a scathing accusation: "The white civ-

ilized man . . . [is] the most ferocious animal on the face of
the earth" (p. 125). Accordingly, the images describing the
"civilized" savages are drawn from the animal world. Visiting
Europeans are "vipers whose sting is destined to poison"
(p. 26). White men are "rapacious hordes" (p. 195). The
"Anglo-Saxons," who exterminated "the greater portion of
the Red race,"[17] are a "hive" (p. 195). Civilized children
cannot play together without "biting" or "scratching one another" (p. 126). The civilized man—who, in *Typee,* is the
European, the Anglo-Saxon, and the American, who, in
short, is white—emerges as an aggressive animal who "by
horrible cruelties has exasperated [the Polynesians] into savages" (p. 27). And if the Polynesian is not provoked into
savagery, he is reduced by the white man's treatment to the
level of a brute. Tommo writes:

Not until I visited Honolulu was I aware of the fact that the small
remnant of the natives had been civilized into draught horses, and
evangelized into beasts of burden. But so it is. They have been
literally broken into the traces, and are harnessed to the vehicles
of their spiritual instructors like so many dumb brutes! [P. 196]

"Dumb brute," noble savage—there is no essential difference. Both roles are creations of the white man. Both deny
the fundamental complexity of character that is a man.

Thus, the white man's impact on Polynesian culture indirectly accounts for Tommo's "inconsistent" portrait of the
Typees—for the facet of their character that critics, such as
James E. Miller, Jr., see as animalistic. Miller argues: "Like
children or animals, their affection and sweetness can be
instantly converted to hate and treachery. The same instinct
and spontaneity which make them so charming and attractive can also render them repulsive and horrible."[18] True, the
Polynesians tend to be mercurial, but the horror and hate
which Miller sees beneath the placid surface of the Polynesians are provoked. The war skirmishes witnessed by Tommo
are acts of self-defense; cannibalism, an act of revenge. The
savage firmness of Kory-Kory and the other Typees, so inconsistent with their loyalty to and benevolent treatment of

Tommo, is provoked by the latter's wish to leave them—a wish constituting a blow to their childlike pride and an implicit violation of their open hospitality. Further, in his desire to reach the sea, Tommo links himself with the threat of the white man who comes by the sea to shatter the peace of the valley. The Typees vividly remember the French sailors and marines who "landed in boats and canoes at the head of the bay" and "on their march back to the sea" set fire "to every house and temple in their route; and a long line of smoking ruins defaced the once-smiling bosom of the valley, and proclaimed to its pagan inhabitants the spirit that reigned in the breasts of Christian soldiers" (p. 26). Treachery and hostility, then, are accounted for as acts stemming from hurt pride, self-preservation, and justifiable distrust. As Tommo himself observes, "Who can wonder at the deadly hatred of the Typees to all foreigners after such unprovoked atrocities?" (p. 26).

The main thrust of Tommo's responses to the dark-skinned primitive and the white civilized worlds is an indictment of the white man as the architect of the wall which separates those worlds. In this connection, he provides ample justification for any feeling of resentment or distrust which the nonwhite may have for the white.

Herman Melville in *Typee* raises no overt cry for racial equality, utters no abolitionist proclamations. The book focuses more on a cultural contrast than on a racial one; but the ironic contrast between the civilized man and the savage man tends to negate the traditional association of whiteness with good and of darkness with evil. Melville does acknowledge that the nonwhite can be beautifully formed, that he can be humane and virtuous, that the white skin is not synonymous with physical and moral superiority—that, in short, skin color is not an automatic index to a man's character. In addition, he suggests that interracial and intercultural hostility is tied to the convenient classifications, the comfortable assumptions one makes of alien worlds. Tommo fears the savage; he admires the savage as noble; but he becomes dimly conscious of the savage as a human, subject to familiar human emotions. At this point in the Melville canon, the dual image of the nonwhite is understandably ambivalent; subsequent books will bring that image into sharp focus.

2.   *OMOO*

> *... It is a curious fact, that the more ignorant and degraded men are, the more contemptuously they look upon those whom they deem their inferiors.*

In *Typee* Tommo-Melville closely observed a people whose innocence and virtue were directly proportionate to their seclusion from the civilized world; likewise, their savagery was linked to the threats posed by that world to their South Pacific Eden. *Typee's* sequel *Omoo: A Narrative of Adventures in the South Seas,* which Anderson calls "perhaps the most strictly autobiographical of all Melville's works,"[1] finds our narrator-wanderer in the crossroads of the Pacific, Tahiti. Here, outside the "garden," he becomes acutely aware of the havoc wreaked on the Polynesians by the white man. Conspicuous in *Omoo* is Melville's repeated use of the word "whites" instead of "civilized man," as tended to be the case in *Typee,* to designate the forces which threatened to defile, and which in fact had considerably tarnished, Tahitian life. *Omoo* also marks the first appearance in Melville's fiction of the black man in the figure of the Negro cook Baltimore, and the first appearance of a savagely vindictive nonwhite who seems to embrace evil for itself alone, the Mowree harpooneer from New Zealand, Bembo. Baltimore is a good-natured, comic

29

character, the butt of practical jokes—in short, the Negro stereotype and a proper candidate for end man in a minstrel show. Bembo, viciously treacherous, brooks no insult from the whites. Both characters offer insights into Melville's growing racial consciousness; both represent forerunners of dark-skinned characters in Melville's later fiction.

Omoo begins where *Typee* leaves off—with Tommo's rescue by the Australian whaler *Julia*. His return to civilization is appropriately ritualized: ". . . Someone removing my tappa cloak slipped on a blue frock in its place; and another, actuated by the same desire to make a civilized mortal of me, flourished about my head a great pair of sheep-shears, to the imminent jeopardy of both ears, and the certain destruction of hair and beard."[2] Properly outfitted and secure behind a civilized ship's bulwarks, he looks back on the Typee Valley, and his first reaction is a sense of loss:

The day was now drawing to a close, and, as the land faded from my sight, I was all alive to the change in my condition. But how far short of our expectations is oftentimes the fulfillment of the most ardent hopes. Safe aboard of a ship—so long my earnest prayer—with home and friends once more in prospect, I nevertheless felt weighed down by a melancholy that could not be shaken off. It was the thought of never more seeing those, who, notwithstanding their desire to retain me a captive, had, upon the whole, treated me so kindly. I was leaving them forever. [P. 7]

The days following that first evening do little to alleviate his misgivings, for the civilized world in which he finds himself consists of a restive, quarrelsome crew—"wild, haggard-looking fellows"—a sickly, ineffectual captain and a drunken first mate. In the Tahitian harbor of Papeete, ten of the crew, including Melville, refuse duty, are charged with mutiny and imprisoned in the local "calabooza." After the *Julia* sails away, the mutineers are permitted to escape. His return to paradise realized, Tommo-Melville becomes "Omoo," a word which "signifies a rover, or rather, a person wandering from one island to another" (p. xiv). What he sees poignantly confirms his feeling the evening of the rescue: that he had left forever the idyllic primitiveness of Polynesian life.

In *Omoo* physical beauty still catches Melville's eye, but his admiration is qualified by his recognition of "the physical degeneracy of the Tahitians as a people" (p. 128). Nonetheless, " . . . among the chiefs, individuals of personable figures are still frequently met with; and occasionally, majestic-looking men, and diminutive women as lovely as the nymphs who, nearly a century ago, swam round the ships of Wallis. In these instances, Tahitian beauty is . . . seducing, . . . the young girls being just such creatures as a poet would picture in the tropics—soft, plump, and dreamy-eyed" (p. 129). The daughter of a chief is a faint echo of Fayaway: "Many heavens were in her sunny eyes; and the outline of that arm of hers, peeping forth from a capricious tappa robe, was the very curve of beauty" (p. 153). Loo, the daughter of Melville's host on the island of Imeeo, has "the most delightful shape— like a bud just blown; and large hazel eyes" (p. 278). With the exception of these brief observations, however, feminine paradise is lost; beauty is overshadowed by character, which, in the case of the Tahitian maidens, is void of the good faith and innocent loyalty of the Typee nymphs. Loo, for example, is "haughty" and responds to Melville and his companion Long Ghost with both contempt and "indolent indifference" (p. 278). The women who come to gaze at the white mutineers from the whaler *Julia* come to laugh and ridicule: "There was little real feeling in them after all" (p. 129). This scene particularly recalls by contrast the warm greeting of the "mermaids" in *Typee.* And in another contrast, this one with the harmonious and communal play of the Typee girls, the Tahitian misses eye one another with envy and scorn.

Physically, the civilized savages of Tahiti are not noble. Melville is struck most by their degeneracy: "I was painfully struck by the considerable number of sickly or deformed persons; undoubtedly made so by a virulent complaint, which, under native treatment, almost invariably affects, in the end, the muscles and bones of the body. In particular, there is a distortion of the back, most unsightly to behold, originating

in a horrible form of the malady" (p. 127). The "virulent
disease which . . . taints the blood of at least two-thirds of
the common people of the island" is so widespread that
Melville prophesies the extinction of the race. With pathos
he records an old chief's lament frequently chanted in a "low,
sad tone by aged Tahitians":

> The palm-tree shall grow,
> The coral shall spread
> But man shall cease. [P. 192]

As for the "Christian" way of life observed in Typee, Melville finds only faint traces in Tahiti. For the most part, moral
degeneracy parallels the physical decay. The custom of making
"bosom friends at the shortest possible notice" has in most
cases "degenerated into a mere mercenary relation" (p. 152).
A Tahitian's professions of friendship turn out to be hollow.
"He was, alas! as sounding brass and a tinkling cymbal; one
of those who make no music unless the clapper be silver"
(p. 157). One recalls the loyal devotion of Tommo's friend
Kory-Kory in *Typee* and sees another departure from the
good life described there. And in contrast to the harmonious
social order of the Typees, the Tahitians are creating a divi-
sion between "better and wealthier orders" and the "common
people" (p. 170). Hypocrisy, too, corrodes the life of the
Polynesians: "After eating bread-fruit at the Eucharist, . . .
several of them, the same night [were] guilty of some sad
derelictions" (p. 177). On another occasion a native girl
tells Melville that she is a church member *here*—pointing to
her mouth—but "by unmistakable gestures" she gave him to
understand "that in certain other respects she is not exactly
a 'mickenaree'" (i.e., church member). The author politely
quotes Pope: "A sad good Christian at the heart/—A very
heathen in the carnal part" (p. 178). In general, then,
Melville depicts the Tahitian Polynesians as people mired
in indolence, fickleness, and licentiousness—a society stripped
of social harmony and individual goodness.

Accounting for the fall of the dusky natives from the innocence of *Typee* to the physical and moral debilitation of

Omoo, Melville indicts the white man. " . . . Bodily afflictions were unknown before the discovery of the islands by the whites" (p. 127). And again, ". . . Depravity among the Polynesians . . . was in a measure unknown before their intercourse with the whites" (p. 188). The white race, in imposing its values on the Polynesians, is responsible for virtually destroying the racial identity of these people: they are deprived of their customs and innocent games, their work, their native dress and their religion, which though "pagan," lacked the hypocrisy and militancy of the missionary brand of Christianity. Little wonder then that Melville concurs with an early voyager, Wheeler, whom he quotes: "How dreadful and appalling . . . the consideration that the intercourse of distant nations should have entailed upon these poor, untutored islanders, a curse unprecedented, and unheard of, in the annals of history" (p. 191). In *Typee* Melville calls the white man "the most ferocious animal on the face of the earth"; in *Omoo,* he defines the extent of that ferocity.

In his biography of Melville, Arvin states that Melville ceased to take pleasure in the spectacle of Polynesian life "at least as he saw it in these haunts of the invading and despoiling whites."[3] True, the delight he evidenced as an observer of the Typees is gone; in its place, however, is a large sympathy for the plight of the natives—and an indirect plea to them to throw off the yoke of white dominance. Describing the horrid effects on the islanders of the white man's disease, Melville narrates the following poignant tale:

Distracted with their sufferings, they [the natives] brought forth their sick before the missionaries, when they were preaching, and cried out, "Lies, Lies! you tell us of salvation; and, behold, we are dying. We want no other salvation than to live in this world. Where are there any saved through your speech? Pomaree [their ruler] is dead; and we are all dying with your cursed diseases. When will you give over?" [P. 191]

"When will you give over?" is a question which carries with it, if not Melville's complete sympathy, then at least his justification and understanding of the nonwhite's occasional re-

bellious and resentful acts against the whites. We are
reminded of Melville's accusation in *Typee*—that the white
man has "exasperated the Polynesians into savages." A similar reciprocity is evident in *Omoo*. A Tahitian girl's cruel
mockery of the white inmates of the Tahitian jail and Loo's
scornfully condescending attitude toward Melville and Long
Ghost are departures from the image of Fayaway; no dexterity of imagination is required, however, to envision the
white sailors' treatment and despoiling of the native girls.
A laugh of ridicule and a glance of scorn are but mild
responses to the bearers of unhappiness and disease. If a
Tahitian friend is faithless, he is only responding to a chain
of deceptions and hypocrisies foisted on him by his white
benefactor. And if the Tahitian regards the white man with
enmity and distrust, he is justified. As Howard observes,
". . . There can be little doubt that [Melville] . . . shared the
natives' resentment at the loss of their formal independence."[4]
Melville's account of an incident that occurred shortly after
his escape from the Typee Valley reflects his position. Approaching an island to procure men for the vacancies in the
crew, a landing party from the *Julia,* "armed with cutlasses,"
sees spearbearing natives standing on the beach. Melville
describes the ensuing events with obvious distaste and anger:

In the end he [the captain] said something which made them
shake their spears; whereupon he fired a pistol among them, which
set the whole party running; while one poor fellow, dropping his
spear and clapping his hand behind him, limped away in a manner which almost made me itch to get a shot at his assailant.
    Wanton acts of cruelty like this are not unusual on the part of
sea captains landing at islands comparatively unknown. Even at
the Pomotu Group, but a day's sail from Tahiti, the islanders
coming down to the shore have several times been fired at by
trading schooners passing through their narrow channels; and this
too as a mere amusement on the part of the ruffians.
    Indeed, it is almost incredible, the light in which many sailors
regard these naked heathens. They hardly consider them human.
[Pp. 24–25]

In view of such treatment, which Melville clearly deplores,
the Polynesians would be inhuman not to respond with dis-

trust and resentment—attitudes which form the basis of rebellion. The pride of a human being, whether dark or white,
cannot endure dehumanization. In this respect, it is interesting to note the pride the Tahitians take in their dark
skin: "A dark complexion in a man . . . is highly esteemed,
as indicating strength of both body and soul." Melville then
cites a saying "of great antiquity" among the natives: "If
dark the cheek of the mother,/The son will sound the war
conch" (p. 129). Thus, the darkness which enhanced the
physical appearance of the Typees, Melville now associates
with "manliness"; tied to the "war conch," that darkness
also recalls the question of the natives to the missionary,
"When will you give over?"

If Melville's adventures in the South Pacific constitute his
discovery of his relationship to other people, then he learns
that "mere imposition of values is neither brotherhood nor
integration."[5] The barrier to "brotherhood," Melville suggests, is the absence of mutual respect which, in turn, becomes
mutual distrust. Further, Melville appears to be developing
an awareness of the dark man as a being capable, on one
hand, of childlike good-humor and affectionate loyalty, and,
on the other, of resentment and latent militancy.

This dual capability of the dark-skinned character is
effectively realized in the persons of Baltimore and Bembo.
Baltimore, a runaway slave from Maryland, is the ship's
black cook, but more significantly, the butt of endless practical jokes. The white crewmen regard him as Mark Twain's
Tom Sawyer regards Nigger Jim—a good-hearted but dull-
witted buffoon to be victimized. The sailors tar his woolly
head, put logs in his bunk, simmer old boots in his cooking
pots, bake cakes of pitch in his oven. "Baltimore's tribulations were indeed sore; there was no peace for him day nor
night" (p. 41). Melville, too, depicts the old cook as a comic
figure, the stereotype "darky." In a gale Baltimore's costume
and Melville's diction in describing the costume emphasize
the ludicrous: ". . . Baltimore always wore what he called his
'gale suit'; among other things, comprising a Sou'-Wester and

a huge pair of well-anointed sea boots, reaching almost to his knees. Thus equipped for a ducking or a drowning, as the case might be, our culinary high priest drew to the slides of his temple, and performed his sooty rites in secret" (p. 59). As interlocutor here, Melville is having fun, and the mock-heroic note is obvious. Baltimore also wears a rope coiled around his middle with the other end fastened to the ship, so afraid is he of being washed overboard. Once, when the cookhouse is flooded, a wave rolls over "pots, pans, and kettles, and even old Baltimore himself, who went breaching along like a porpoise," and is left "high and dry on the after-hatch: his extinguished pipe still between his teeth, and almost bitten in two." Baltimore is the proper end man; as for the audience-crew, they "did nothing but roar at his calamity" (p. 59). Melville's closing the incident by noting the callousness of the crew suggests an attitude which sets him apart from his mates. He can "josh" Baltimore, but the Melville sympathy is here too: "Poor fellow! he was altogether too good-natured. Say what they will about easy-tempered people, it is far better, on some accounts, to have the temper of a wolf" (p. 41).

If Baltimore lacks the wolfish temper, Bembo, the "dark, moody, savage" harpooneer, does not. A scowler, "he was all compact, and under his swart, tattooed skin, the muscles worked like steel rods. Hair, crisp and coal-black, curled over shaggy brows, and ambushed small, intense eyes, always on the glare. In short, he was none of your effeminate barbarians" (p. 71). As for Bembo's heart, it is "irreclaimably savage," his rage, "demoniac." In a fight Bembo tries to bite the throat of a white seaman. Subdued, "he lay glaring and writhing on the deck." Later he tries to destroy the entire crew by steering the ship toward a coral reef. Also emphasizing Bembo's savagery is the story of his killing a whale. He is pictured bounding on the whale's back, plunging his harpoon in foam and fury, lashing up a "whirlpool of blood and brine." Possessed of the "blood-thirsty propensities" of New Zealanders, Bembo "was a wild one after a fish." As might be expected, the crew "distrusted and feared him. Nor were these feelings unreciprocated" (p. 71).

Melville does not condone Bembo's savagery; he does, however, provide justification for it. The fight[6] was precipitated by Sidney Ben's "casting some illiberal reflections on the Mowree's maternal origin, which the latter had been long enough among sailors to understand as in the highest degree offensive" (p. 87). Further, Sidney Ben strikes the first blow. According to Melville, the fight is "even"; yet the entire crew haul Bembo off his assailant, after which they rejoice "at seeing him thus humbled" and berate him "for a cannibal and a coward" (p. 88). This humiliation, then, triggers Bembo's attempt to destroy the ship: "His only motive could have been, a desire to revenge the contumely heaped upon him the night previous" (pp. 92–93). When again subdued after his unsuccessful attempt to wreck the ship, Bembo is rushed by the crew, who shout 'Down with him!' 'Strike him down!' 'Hang him at the mainyard!' Alone, his sheath knife glittering above his head, Bembo awaits the massed assault. Melville does not conceal his wonder at and admiration for Bembo's fierce courage: "But he stood unmoved, and, for a single instant, they [the crew] absolutely faltered" (p. 91). Even the wild account of the butchering of the whale occurs *after* "the taunts of the seamen may have maddened the Mowree" (p. 72). For all his ruthlessness, Bembo has a right to defy; Melville recognizes this right in his final estimate of the Mowree: "Such a man, or devil, if you will, was Bembo" (p. 72).

"Man, or devil"? Perhaps qualities of both are vital to the complete being. Unlike Baltimore, whose good nature and subservience earn for him unending tribulation, Bembo responds to indignities with a pride which, though savage, is also courageously human. We recall Melville's incredulous observation that sailors consider the natives as "hardly human," and we recognize in Bembo's rebellion a terrifying assertion of his manhood and of his self-respect. Baltimore may be an amusing figure with whom a sensitive Melville can sympathize, but he is not a man. He is one image of the dark-skinned characters in Melville's fiction. The other is the savage Bembo—too much a "wolf" perhaps but a figure who, at least, commands respect.

3. *MARDI*

> *Civilization has not ever been the brother of equality. Freedom was born among the wild eyries in the mountains; and barbarous tribes have sheltered under her wings, when the enlightened people of the plain have nestled under different pinions.*

In *Mardi and A Voyage Thither,* his third published work, Melville retains the South Seas setting of *Typee* and *Omoo* but abandons the role of observer reporting his travels. Stung perhaps by the attacks on his veracity, attacks probably directed toward his denunciation of missionary activities in his first two works, Melville prefaces his novel with this sarcastic comment: "Not long ago, having published two narratives of voyages in the Pacific, which, in many quarters, were received with incredulity, the thought occurred to me, of indeed writing a romance of Polynesian adventure, and publishing it as such; to see whether the fiction might not, possibly, be received for a verity: in some degree the reverse of my previous experience."[1] As "a romance of Polynesian adventure," *Mardi* presents complications so far as Melville's racial attitudes are concerned. No longer, for instance, does Melville as reporter directly state his observations of the Polynesians. Instead, the reader must rely on the dramatic

presentation of those characters in order to discern any relationship to the dark-skinned figures of the earlier books.
Further, the "adventure" tale promised in the preface is never
fully realized. Before we are one-fourth of the way through
the text, the narrative blends into a voyage both allegorical
and philosophical—a voyage which is a vehicle for Melville's
"criticism of life."[2] In short, "We find in *Mardi*," as John
Bernstein states, "the sudden metamorphosis of Melville from
a writer of comparatively simple and straightforward travel
adventures to an author deeply committed to symbolism as a
technique whose major concern is with the most profound
and pressing issues facing mankind."[3]

Throughout, point of view is, to say the least, perplexing.
The original narrator, a restless American sailor who deserts
a whaler at sea, is nameless; as the book approaches allegory,
he assumes the role of Taji, a demigod from the sun. In the
latter half of the work, he fades into a listener, and the narrative is conducted by the voices of the statesman Media, the
poet Yoomy, the historian Mohi, and, most of all, the philosopher Babbalanja. To find Melville's voice in such a
Pandora's box is not easy; metaphysical, social, political, and
religious ideas are juggled, weighed, examined, channeled
into ambiguous conclusions. Nonetheless, the ideas are there,
and we sense Melville's groping with the world of the mind.
As Warner Berthoff observes, "In *Mardi* we feel Melville's
thoughts, and his very motives to thinking, taking form and
gathering momentum, very little according to the require-
ments either of theme or of structure, but very much according to the progressive inclinings and urgings of his own immediate apprehension."[4] Accordingly, to attribute to Melville
a fixed idea, and especially a specific conclusion, with regard
to any issue raised in *Mardi* would be dangerous. A close
examination of the text, however, not only reveals Melville's
continued interest in the relationship between the dark and
white races but also suggests an amplification of thematic
considerations already raised in the chapters on *Typee* and
Omoo. First, in the "adventure" part of the romance are two

Polynesian characters, Samoa and Annatoo, who in appearance, character, and action recall the duality of the dark-skinned natives noted in the preceding chapter. Emphasizing this duality is the background information provided for another character—the white maiden Yillah. Second, in the allegorical voyage, Melville gives considerable attention to the tribe of Hamo in Vivenza—the Negro in America.

In the fashion of *Typee* and *Omoo, Mardi* begins as an adventure yarn set in the South Pacific, narrated by a sailor seeking escape. In this case, tormented by the monotony of the whaling voyage and repelled by the prospect of a right whale hunt near the Arctic Circle, the narrator, along with a faithful and taciturn Norwegian, Jarl, steals a whale boat, the *Chamois,* and abandons ship. Hoping to reach a chain of distant "Westward isles," they sail for days, plagued by lack of water, a scorching sun, and maddening calms. At last they sight the sail of the brigantine *Parki,* from all appearances a ghost ship. After boarding her and conducting an eerie night search for clues to her mystery, they discover in the light of morning that the vessel is occupied by two Polynesians— Samoa, a native of the Navigator Isles, and his termagant wife Annatoo, a native of a distant, anonymous island to the westward. Implicit in Melville's handling of this pair is the same question raised in connection with Bembo in *Omoo*— "man, or devil?" At the same time, they are comic figures described in the same mock-heroic tone as was Baltimore of *Omoo.*

Physically, Samoa and Annatoo are far removed from the attractive Polynesians of the Typee Valley. Samoa, in appearance, is more "devil" than "man." Although tall and dark, "an obelisk in stature," Samoa is "a very devil to behold" (p. 66). Serving as sheath for his knife, Samoa's ear lobe is so elongated by the weapon's weight that it droops upon his shoulder. The middle cartilage of his nose sports a polished nail. No small part of his ugliness is the stump of an amputated arm. Tending the tiller at night, he presents an appalling aspect: "His large opal eyes were half open; and

turned toward the light of the binnacle, gleamed between the
lids like bars of flame. And added to all, was his giant stature
and savage lineaments" (p. 109). As for Annatoo, the narrator (evidently a chivalrous soul) spares us the painful details: "I can make no pleasing portrait of the dame; for as in
most ugly subjects, flattering would but make the matter
worse. Furthermore, unalleviated ugliness should ever go un-
painted, as something unnecessary to duplicate" (p. 99).
Physically, then, our Polynesian couple, particularly Samoa,
are stereotype savages, complete with lurid eyes and bone in
nose. (One is almost disappointed in the absence of filed
teeth.) At any rate, they are cast in the physical mold of
Bembo ("none of your effeminate barbarians"), and they
recall the threatening dark savages in the "escape" chapters
of *Typee*.

Intensifying their savage appearance are the "animal"
images attached to them. Samoa is a "fiery steed" (specifically, "Bucephalus," Alexander's war horse, which "when he
patted, he preferred holding by the bridle"), a "wild buffalo,"
a "tawny leopard," and, on one occasion, a "Newfoundland
dog."[5] Annatoo is a veritable zoo. Her nails are "talons." She
is a "tigress" and a "hornet." In the hold she is "wont to coil
herself away, like a garter-snake under a stone." Or else she
is "forever on the prowl." Let it suffice that the images, together with the hideous physical portraits, mark these nonwhites as subhuman savages.

But, as the narrator of *Mardi* elsewhere states, "To be called
one thing, is oftentimes to be another" (p. 269); an examination of Samoa's actions reveals a "man" as well as a "devil."
Interestingly enough, even a part of his physical appearance,
his style of tattooing, suggests a dual character. The marks
cover "a vertical half of his person, from crown to sole; the
other side being free from the slightest stain. Thus clapped
together . . . he looked like a union of the unmatched moieties
of two distinct beings. . . . When he turned round upon you
suddenly, you thought you saw some one else, not him whom
you had been regarding before" (pp. 98–99). This "someone

else" is more "human" than his physical features would suggest.

Samoa and Annatoo are the sole survivors of a thirty-man crew (only four of whom were white men) butchered in a sneak attack by two Cholos[6] and a tribe of natives. During the ferocious attack Samoa displayed both presence of mind and stark heroism. His arm mangled by two savages, he managed to escape below where "while yet the uproar of butchery prevailed, he quietly bound up his arm; then laying on the transom the captain's three loaded muskets, undauntedly awaited an assault" (p. 70). The picture recalls Bembo's waiting "unmoved" the rush of the massed crew of the *Julia.* Just as the attackers were about to wreck the *Parki,* Samoa alone launched a counterattack which succeeded in driving them from the ship. Instantly he took charge, preparing the *Parki* for sail to escape the threatening reef. Shooting by the reef, he was not yet safe, for, turning, he saw in pursuit a whaleboat manned by the Cholos and several islanders. "His shattered arm in a hempen sling, Samoa stood at the helm, the muskets reloaded, and planted full before him on the binnacle" (p. 71). Again the emphasis is on fierce bravery; this time, however, the courage is underscored by the motive: retaliation. "Maddened by the sight [of the pursuers], and perhaps thinking more of revenge for the past, than of security for the future . . . Samoa rested his muskets on the bulwarks, and taking long, sure aim, discharged them, one by one at the advancing foe" (p. 72). No cowardly "heathen" fleeing in panic from superior numbers and certain death, Samoa is a figure who, oblivious to pain, defiantly and deliberately strikes back. In this episode Samoa emerges as a "man." The "devil," however, is not submerged. The ruthlessness and completeness of his revenge constitute sufficient testimony to the hellishness of which Melville's dark-skinned characters seem to be capable when provoked:

"Load away now, and take thy revenge, my fine fellow," said Samoa to himself. But not yet. Seeing all at his mercy, and having none, he quickly laid his fore-topsail to the mast; "hove to" the

brigantine; and opened fire anew upon the boat; every swell of
the sea heaving it nearer and nearer. Vain all efforts to escape.
The wounded man [in the boat] paddled wildly with his hands;
the dead one rolled from side to side; and the Cholo, seizing the
solitary oar, in his frenzied heedlessness, spun the boat round and
round; while all the while shot followed shot, Samoa firing as
fast as Annatoo could load. At length both Cholo and savage fell
dead upon their comrades, canting the boat over sideways till
well-nigh awash; in which manner she drifted off. [Pp. 72–73]

Devil? Perhaps. But considering the butchery of the *Parki*'s
crew, the mutilation of Samoa's arm, and his instinct to sur-
vive, Samoa's savage vindictiveness is justified. Further, in
the absence of any other "savage" act on his part, his evil (so
far as evil may be related to the ruthless violence of the nonwhite) is motivated by revenge. Like his predecessor Bembo,
Samoa may be "wolfish," but he elicits both awe and respect.
The narrator concedes as much and, at the same time, is aware
of Samoa's duality: ". . . Though he deferred to me . . . he
was, notwithstanding, a man who, without precisely meditat-
ing mischief, could upon occasion act an ugly part. But of his
courage, and savage honor . . . I had little doubt" (p. 96).

Even though the narrator "assumed the decided air of a
master" (p. 90) toward Samoa, the latter is not the deferen-
tial and subservient follower that one might expect an "inferior" native to be. At times he treats his white companions as
he had been treated by them, thus echoing the reciprocal
nature of race relations evident in *Omoo*. Once on land,
Samoa assumes toward the whites, particularly the Norwegian
Jarl, the role of superior and master: ". . . Concerning himself and the Skyeman [Jarl], the tables were turned. At sea,
Jarl had been the oracle. . . . But our craft high and dry, the
Upoluan [Samoa] lifted his crest as the erudite pagan; master
of Gog and Magog, expounder of all things heathenish and
obscure" (p. 172). On another occasion a group of natives,
acting as hosts to the refugees from the *Parki*, laugh at Jarl's
appearance. Samoa roars louder than any: ". . . He seemed
rejoiced at the opportunity of turning upon us the ridicule,
which as a barbarian among whites, he himself had so often

experienced" (p. 181). Like the cynical maidens and faith-less friends of Tahiti, Samoa in his native element respects white men in proportion to the respect they accord him in their native environment. Perhaps Jarl's preposterous hat is as humorous to Samoa as the latter's ear is to Jarl. The narrator himself, sounding much like the Melville of *Moby-Dick,* sup-plies the answer to those who would question and feel supe-rior to "savage" acts and appearances: "Away with our stares and grimaces. The New Zealander's tattooing is not a prodigy; nor the Chinaman's way an enigma. No custom is strange; no creed is absurd; no foe, but who will in the end prove a friend" (pp. 12–13). In another instance, the American-seaman narrator of *Mardi* anticipates the brotherhood theme of *Moby-Dick.* In speaking of the ancestry of Jarl, he de-clares: ". . . All generations are blended: and heaven and earth of one kin: the hierarchies of seraphs in the uttermost skies; the thrones and principalities in the zodiac; the shades that roam throughout space; the nations and families, flocks and folds of the earth; one and all, brothers in essence—oh, be we then brothers indeed!" (p. 12).

Other qualities, too, serve to raise Samoa above the stereo-type savage: his seamanship, his position of subordinate offi-cer in charge of all the natives aboard the *Parki,* his patience in the face of the shrewish Annatoo's harangues, his pride in his island birthplace—all combine to create a character who, notwithstanding the dangling ear and pierced nose, is in ac-tion and character a "man."

As for ugly Annatoo, even though "possessed by some scores of devils, perpetually inciting her to mischief" (p. 113), she is clearly the comic relief in the adventure part of *Mardi.* Cast as the termagant wife constantly haranguing her be-leaguered husband, she is given the complete mock-heroic treatment. Typical of the mock-epic tone in which their "con-nubial bliss" is related is the following passage, complete with epic simile: ". . . In capacity of wife, Annatoo the dame, ac-companied in the brigantine, Samoa her lord. Now, as Antony flew to the refuse embraces of Caesar, so Samoa solaced himself in the arms of this discarded fair one. And the sequel was the same. For not harder the life Cleopatra led my fine frank friend, poor Mark, than Queen Annatoo did lead this captive of her bow and her spear" (p. 69). During one of their frequent separations, she is "Antonia" and poor Samoa, her "Belisarius": "Thus did the pair make a divorce of it; the lady going upon a separate maintenance—and Belisarius resuming his bachelor loneliness. In the captain's state room, all cold and comfortless, he slept; his lady . . . retiring to her forecastle boudoir; beguiling the hours in saying her paternosters, and tossing over and assorting her ill-gotten trinkets and finery; like Madame De Maintenon dedicating her last days and nights to continence and calicoes" (p. 81). Annatoo, then, is treated in the manner of that "culinary high priest," Baltimore—an amusing (but, in her case, annoying) diversion relieving the monotony of an equatorial voyage.

Like her husband, however, Annatoo occasionally steps out of her role of Polynesian shrew and thus acquires a degree of "humanness." It is Annatoo who is assigned the task of amputating Samoa's arm with a blunt ax. Her "industry," united with Samoa's seamanship, saves them from smashing into a shoal. She is also "quite an expert" as helmsman. While commenting on her ugliness, the narrator concedes: "Yet how avoid admiring those Penthesilian qualities which so signally had aided Samoa, in wresting the *Parki* from its treacherous captors" (pp. 90–91). And, in spite of her sulking and tantrums, this "indefatigable and inquisitive dame" is missed by the narrator: ". . . Alas, poor Annatoo. . . . And bethinking me of the hard fate that so soon overtook thee, I almost repent what has already and too faithfully been portrayed" (p. 115). Like Samoa, Annatoo is not only a devil (albeit a comic one) but also a human, in many respects a typical woman to whom the narrator responds as one must respond to such creatures— with both exasperation and affection.

With the death of Annatoo, the "adventure" portion of *Mardi* approaches its climax—the narrator's abduction of the ethereal white maiden Yillah. In a large ceremonial canoe a native priest, Aleema, and his sons are bearing Yillah to be sacrificed to their pagan gods. Determined to rescue a maiden in distress (or selfishly to acquire the companionship of a woman), the narrator succeeds in killing the priest and fleeing with the girl. Landing at Odo, an island ruled by King Media, the narrator deceives his hosts by assuming the identity of Taji, one of their demigods. He then retires with Yillah to a blissful bower, only to find her one day mysteriously gone. Taji and four members of the royal court—King Media, the philosopher Babbalanja, the poet Yoomy, and the historian Mohi—set off to search all of Mardi (the world) to find Yillah, who, in the framework of the allegory, says Bruce Franklin, "incarnates the object of all quests (Astraea, the Absolute, the Ideal, Happiness, Truth, the Pearl, the beckoning fair one)."[7] Significantly, Samoa refuses to join the quest. His decision emphasizes his earthiness and practicality and thus underscores Taji's search for the impossible.[8] In the remainder of the book, action is limited to the wanderings of the searchers and to the occasional appearance of Aleema's three remaining sons, who are determined to avenge their father's murder. For the most part, however, plot is subordinate to a rambling exchange of political, social, religious, and philosophical views. Nevertheless, the allegorical *Mardi* provides echoes of the "revenge" theme discussed in connection with Bembo and Samoa, and thus offers insights into Melville's observations of nonwhites.

Although a "comely set" with complexions of "gold sherry," Aleema and his sons, Yillah's captors, are particularly ferocious. When the refugees from the *Parki* first approach the sacred canoe carrying Yillah to her sacrifice, they are met with a "storm of vociferations" and brandished spears and clubs. Everything about Yillah's captors is sinister. Aleema's face is "overcast with a ferocious expression" (p. 132) when he recalls his experience aboard a Western vessel. His sons, who pursue Taji throughout all of Mardi, are "specter-like" with faces "like skulls" (p. 306). Their eyes are "deep, dry, crater-like hollows, lurid with flames" (p.

307). They are "skeletons" who pronounce a bloodthirsty
curse on Taji: ". . . White curses upon thee! Bleached be thy
soul with our hate! Living, our brethren cursed thee; and
dying, dry-lipped, they cursed thee again. . . . Thy blood, their
thirst would have slaked" (pp. 306–07). Again, they threaten,
". . . We rave and raven for you; and your white heart will
we have!" (p. 308). From their deathlike appearance to their
repelling curses, Aleema's sons are harrowing figures of evil.

Their viciousness, however, is not that conventionally associated with the barbarous savage; their evil is not for evil's
sake. Instead, their hatred, like Bembo's and Samoa's, results
from what the white Taji did to them; thus, revenge precipi-
tates their ferocious pursuit. The sons declare to Taji, "They
[their brothers] died not through famishing for water, but for
revenge upon thee!" (p. 307). Taji, then, is the initial of-
fender. According to Bernstein, "As the result of his use of
violence, Taji succeeds in liberating Yillah, but only at the
cost of killing Aleema, which is a crime, as the narrator himself readily admits."[9] And if he has freed Yillah, the question
must be asked, "For what?" She becomes the captive of Taji's
deceit and, subsequently, the captive of the sensual and evil
Queen Hautia.

Few critics are charitable in their estimation of Taji. Stern
calls him a "blasphemer";[10] Franklin, a "temperamental
fraud";[11] Miller, "the individual who will not accept his human guilt."[12] F. O. Matthiessen sees the loss of Yillah as a
"disaster" resulting from "an initial act of evil"[13] on Taji's
part. Thus, the whole episode echoes the pattern of *Omoo*:
the white offends; the nonwhite retaliates. The alternative for
Aleema's sons is to accept the murder of their father and a
blasphemous blow against their faith, in effect, to become
patient Baltimores enduring the insult and violence of their
white assailant. No, like Bembo, they will have vengeance;
though, as Stern points out, "their hatred and thirst for vengeance is a . . . hatred that parches and shrivels and bleaches
what it touches,"[14] it carries with it an all-too-human dedication which underscores Taji's selfishness. Contrary to what the

white sailors of *Omoo* may think, the South Sea native can be human and, accordingly, be driven by the same sense of injury and purpose which the white man can feel.

Taji's was not the first act of treachery inflicted on Aleema's people; other whites established a precedent. Relating Yillah's history, the sons tell of "a mighty canoe, full of beings, white, like this murderer Taji," which landed at their island. The whites (who included Yillah and her parents) were treated royally—"worshipped as gods," "feasted all over the land," showered "with offerings of fruit and flowers." Their hospitality recalls the warmth of the Typees and, to a lesser degree, that of the Tahitians. And how did the white gods repay the natives' faith? The sons continue the tale: "All went well between our people and the gods, till at last, they slew three of our countrymen, charged with stealing from their great canoe" (pp. 307–08). Little wonder that the most evil curse Aleema's sons can pronounce is a "white" curse. Once again, the question of *Typee*—who is savage, the civilized man or the native? —is central to this episode. In a pattern which seems to be becoming typical of race relations in Melville's fiction, the nonwhites, provoked by white crimes, justifiably retaliate: "Our warriors retired to the hills, brooding over revenge. Three days went by; when by night, descending to the plain, in silence they embarked; gained the great vessel, and slaughtered every soul but Yillah" (p. 308). Melville makes abundantly clear in this narrative that the white man has "exasperated the Polynesians into savages."

When the white man is not provoking the Polynesian into savagery, he is reducing the black man to the state of a "brute." Such is the discovery of the questers in *Mardi* when, in their search for Yillah, they visit America or, as it is called in the allegory, Vivenza. At the entrance to Vivenza stands an arch on which immense "hieroglyphics" boldly proclaim: "In this republican land all men are born free and equal." In much smaller characters, however, is the qualifier—"except the tribe of Hamo"—an addition which, Media quickly declares, "nullifies" the larger declaration (pp. 512–13). Ample evidence testifies to the truth of the smaller hieroglyphics. "A man with a collar round his neck, and the red marks of stripes upon his back," raises a standard, "correspondingly striped" (p. 515), over the "federal temple of freedom" which, itself, is "the handiwork of slaves" (p. 528). A visit to the extreme south of Vivenza reveals "under a burning sun, hundreds of collared men . . . toiling in trenches. . . . Standing grimly over these, were men unlike them; armed with long thongs which descended upon the toilers and made wounds" (pp. 531–32).

The defense by the overseer (John Calhoun) of slavery and the questers' shocked reaction to it constitute a bitterly satirical commentary on Melville's country. To the slaveholder, the blacks, or the tribe of Hamo, are not men; "Their souls have been bred out of [them]; as the instinct of scent is killed in pointers" (p. 532). Accordingly, he defends their bondage as one might defend a zoo: "Are they not fed, clothed, and cared for? [They] have no thoughts, no cares" (p. 533). Babbalanja, however, prefers to regard the slaves as beings deprived of their right to be men: "Thoughts and cares are life, and liberty, and immortality!" (p. 533). And again, "Some seem happy: yet not as men. Unmanned, they know not what they are" (p. 534). Even King Media wonders about the "humanness" of the slaves: "Surely this being has flesh that is warm. . . . I swear he is a man" (p. 532). Man? Animal? The slave himself responds, "Under the lash, I believe my masters and account myself a brute; but in my dreams, bethink myself an angel" (p. 532). Just as the Polynesian is a savage under white harassment, the American Negro is a brute under the white man's lash. Perhaps *Mardi* provides a partial answer to the question Melville raises about Bembo—"man, or devil?" To be a man is to think, to care, to dream, and to be free from exploitation and insult. To be a man is to be free from the lash which reduces humans to brutes; with the lash remaining, however, the "angel" the slave envisions himself could well be an avenging angel.

Certainly the questers see just cause for violent upheaval.

Yoomy cries, "Oh beings as ourselves, how my stiff arm shivers to avenge you!" (p. 533). His indignation is a call to arms: ". . . Were there no other way and should their masters not relent, all honest hearts must cheer this tribe of Hamo on; though they cut their chains with blades thrice edged, and gory to the haft! 'Tis right to fight for freedom, whoever be the thrall" (p. 533). The historian Mohi prophesies, "These South savannahs may yet prove battlefields" (p. 533). The aristocratic and caustic Media, ever quick to castigate the hypocrisy of this "republican" land, murmurs, ". . . Were these serfs to rise, and fight for it [freedom]; like dogs, they would be hunted down by her [freedom's] pretended sons!" (p. 533).

As the chapter on the south of Vivenza draws to a close and the initial shock of seeing men as collared brutes subsides, the questers agree that a prudent remedy cannot be found and that, ultimately, Vivenza must solve its own problem. Moderation is urged; as Babbalanja says to Yoomy, ". . . So far as feeling goes, your sympathies are not more hot than mine; but for these serfs you would cross spears; yet I would not. Better present woes for some, than future woes for all" (pp. 533–34). Matthiessen sees in the philosopher's remark Melville's making "a plea for moderation on the part of the North in order to preserve the Union."[15] Willard Thorp calls Melville's conclusion to the chapter "not the words of an Abolitionist."[16] True, Babbalanja advocates discretion so far as full-scale war is concerned, but he also declares, "In all things, man's own battles, man himself must fight" (p. 533). Thus, if, as Matthiessen suggests, Babbalanja is Melville's voice,[17] then this last comment would be an indirect justification of Bembo's savagery in *Omoo*. It is Babbalanja who, as their craft fights through a violent storm off the coast of Africa, foresees the storm of just retaliation that will strike America: "Thus [in reference to the lightning and the storm-lashed sea] oh Vivenza! retribution works! Though long delayed, it comes at last—Judgment, with all her bolts!" (p.

554). Perhaps he, too, dreams of the slave as an "angel"—the avenging variety.

It might be well, at this point, to quote at length Babbalanja's angry indictment of slavery as evil:

. . . Sin it is, no less;—a blot, foul as the crater-pool of hell; it puts out the sun at noon; it parches all fertility; and, conscience or no conscience—ere he die—let every master who wrenches bond-babe from mother, that the nipple tear; unwreathes the arms of sisters; or cuts the holy unity in twain; till apart fall man and wife, like one bleeding body cleft:—let that master thrice shrive his soul; take every sacrament; on his bended knees give up the ghost;—yet shall he die forever damned. [Pp. 534–35]

To Babbalanja's damning of the slaveholder must be added Yoomy's pity for the slaves. About Africa, he cries:

Poor land! curst of man . . . ! how thou faintest for thy children torn from thy soil to till a stranger's. . . . Oh, tribe of Hamo! thy cup of woe so brims, that soon it must overflow upon the land which holds ye thralls. No misery born of crime, but spreads and poisons wide. Suffering hunteth sin, as the gaunt hound the hare, and tears it in the greenest brakes. [p. 554]

In the "Supplement" to *The Battle-Pieces and Aspects of War,* Melville notes that the "implied end" of the Civil War "was the erecting in our advanced century of an Anglo-American empire based upon the systematic degradation of man."[18] In *Mardi* his hatred of a system that tyrannizes and brutalizes men and his compassion for those brutalized— "Humanity cries out against this vast enormity" (p. 534)— anticipate that later conviction. As John Freeman states, "Here, indeed, in the satire of the South the satirist forgets his assumption and the heart speaks; and a wisdom and humanity that come not with ironic laughter are plainly heard in all that is said."[19] As to whether the attitudes expressed by Babbalanja and Yoomy are really Melville's, let it suffice that the pity in *Mardi* is the same expressed for the disease-ridden Tahitians of *Omoo* and that the anger is the same unleashed toward the white despoilers of Polynesian life who see the dark-skinned man as an object of ridicule, exploitation, and abuse. Looking back on the Civil War, Melville conceded "that emancipation was accomplished not by deliberate legislation; only through agonized violence could so mighty a result be effected."[20] Although open rebellion may not be the solution to Vivenza's evil in *Mardi,* Melville could "understand" such rebellion, for at its base would be man's assertion of his right to be human. It is inconceivable that Melville would "except the tribe of Hamo" from his land of equality and freedom.

4. *REDBURN*

*Now, whenever we discover a dislike in us,
toward anyone, we should ever be a little suspicious of ourselves.*

Redburn, Melville's fourth work, transports the reader
from the South Pacific to the North Atlantic, from the luxuriant beauty of Polynesian isles to the fetid squalor of the
Liverpool slums. It, too, is a quest, not of a man seeking an
Eden or of a disenchanted sailor pursuing an ethereal maiden
incarnating all goals, but of a boy unconsciously seeking his
identity as a young man. That voyager on the *Highlander,*
a merchant ship bound for Liverpool, is Wellingborough Redburn; the narrator of the novel bearing his name, he departs
New York a naive boy and returns a reasonably mature
young man. Like Hawthorne's young Robin in "My Kinsman,
Major Molineux," Redburn passes from innocence through
experience to knowledge; and, like Robin, he plunges into the
world and emerges, potentially, a "shrewd youth." Redburn's
attitudes through the course of the narrative undergo a change
paralleling his growing awareness of reality. Accordingly,
when he describes and reacts to nonwhites aboard the *Highlander,* what must be considered is whether that reaction
comes from the self-centered and relatively closed mind of
the youth or from the sympathetic and more tolerant mind

of the experienced voyager. Melville's treatment of the dark races in *Redburn* cannot be divorced from the narrator's aberrations and changes.

At the beginning of the novel, Wellingborough Redburn has, with embellishments, Henry James's "great American disease"—a romantic yearning, inspired by books and paintings, for foreign places: "fine old lands, full of mossy cathedrals and churches, and long, narrow, crooked streets without sidewalks, and lined with strange houses."[1] Crowding his imagination are images of "fountains, and courts, and gardens, with long lines of thick foliage cut into fantastic doors and windows, and towers and pinnacles," or "rural scenes, full of fine skies, pensive cows standing up to the knees in water, and shepherd-boys and cottages in the distance, half concealed in vineyards and vines" (p. 6). With "this continual dwelling upon foreign associations," he sees himself fated to be "a great voyager" (p. 7). The sea, too, assumes in young Redburn's romantic mind the coloring of old prints. In his vague dreamings, "sunburnt sea-captains . . . smoking cigars, and talking about Havanna, London, and Calcutta," sail sea-worn crafts "with high, cosy bulwarks, and rakish masts and yards" over waves "toasted brown" or "blue as Sicily skies." More than anything else, what activates his romantic longings is a delicate glass ship safely moored within a glass case in one corner of the sitting room. A portion of Redburn's decription will suffice to illustrate the childlike wonder with which he regards this image of life at sea:

Not to speak of the tall masts, and yards, and rigging of this famous ship, among whose mazes of spun-glass I used to rove in imagination, till I grew dizzy at the main-truck, I will only make mention of the people on board of her. They, too, were all of glass, as beautiful little glass sailors as anybody ever saw, with hats and shoes on, just like living men, and curious blue jackets with a sort of ruffle round the bottom. Four or five of these sailors were very nimble little chaps, and were mounting up the rigging with very long strides. [P. 8]

The glass ship and the pretty glass sailors represent a telling index to Redburn's general ignorance of the actual world and, more specifically, of life at sea.

Dominant in Wellingborough's delicate glass world is the inflated and self-centered image of himself as a much-traveled man to be regarded with awe:

... I frequently fell into long reveries about distant voyages and travels, and thought how fine it would be to be able to talk about remote and barbarous countries; with what reverence and wonder people would regard me, if I had just returned from the coast of Africa or New Zealand; how dark and romantic my sunburnt cheeks would look; how I would bring home with me foreign clothes of a rich fabric and princely make, and wear them up and down the streets, and how grocers' boys would turn back their heads to look at me as I went by. [P. 5]

Redburn's itch to wander is a striving not so much for experience as for self-glorification. His world is small; it consists very much of himself. One can hardly disagree with Bernstein's estimate of Redburn as "the youngest and most completely naive and unformed of Melville's protagonists."[2]

Redburn's naiveté is underscored by his conception of himself. He is a snob, but the snobbery is obviously a cover for an inadequacy—his ignorance of the actual world. He relishes having "previously associated with persons of a very discreet life" (p. 49). A member of both the "Juvenile Total Abstinence Association" and the "Anti-Smoking Society," he piously condescends to feel a readily manufactured pity toward his crude mates:

Yes, I now began to look on them with a sort of incipient love; but more with an eye of pity and compassion, as men of naturally gentle and kind dispositions, whom only hardships, and neglect, and ill-usage had made outcasts from good society; and not as villains who loved wickedness for the sake of it, and would persist in wickedness, even in Paradise, if they ever got there. And I called to mind a sermon I had once heard in a church in behalf of sailors, when the preacher called them strayed lambs from the fold, and compared them to poor lost children, babes in the wood, orphans without fathers and mothers. [P. 47]

The "compassion" confessed here reflects the sanctimonious air of the uninitiated. Redburn has neatly categorized people in accord with his childhood dreams or with the built-in prejudice of a "discreet life." As preconceptions similar to the above are, one by one, destroyed, Wellingborough receives his share of Melville's ironic barbs.

Redburn's naiveté and his air of superiority are quite evident in his early responses to the blacks aboard the *Highlander*. Even before he ships, an incident occurs which accurately marks his attitude toward "inferiors" and which alerts the reader to the type of judgment Redburn is prone to exercise. Penniless and hungry, he tries to appease his aching stomach by filling it up with water; but he "had much ado to get down the water; for it tasted warm; and the tumbler had an ugly flavor." Why? He continues, ". . . [A] negro had been drinking some spirits out of it [tumbler] just before" (p. 25). Now, whether his qualms can be attributed to the "spirits" or to the Negro's having drunk from the same glass is difficult to say; but in view of his being "grateful" that he is "different from" base sailors, one must be suspicious of Redburn's level of tolerance for blacks.

At any rate, the portraits of the two blacks aboard the *Highlander*—the cook, Mr. Thompson, and the steward, Lavender—are sketched with the fastidious hand of the "upright" young man. It is quite apparent that Redburn's view of blacks is derived from the same source as are his dreams of life at sea. His preconceptions place the blacks on a level somewhat below that of human beings. Finding himself without a cup, he thinks of borrowing one from the black cook, "but he looked so cross and ugly then, that the sight of him almost frightened the idea" (p. 40) out of Redburn. Completing the "bogeyman" picture of Thompson, Redburn notes that he is "suspicious-looking." As for the cook's color, Wellingborough observes:

It was well for him that he was a black cook, for I have no doubt his colour kept us from seeing his dirty face; I never saw him wash but once, and that was at one of his own soup pots one dark night when he thought no one saw him. What induced him to be washing his face then, I never could find out; but I suppose he must have suddenly waked up, after dreaming about some real estate on his cheeks. [P. 43]

The quip at the conclusion of this passage is reminiscent of Melville's treatment of Baltimore, but most pronounced is the fear and distaste bred of ignorance which Redburn shows. One could argue that Redburn is simply objecting to uncleanliness; on no occasion, however, does he observe dirt on his white mates, most of whom are the dregs of humanity. It is conceivable that the foul-tasting water incident and Redburn's initial view of the cook reflect the same thing—a view of the black as, at least, disagreeably unclean, and, at most, repelling.

Wellingborough, however, has not yet dipped his hand in a tar bucket, not yet scaled the main mast to loosen the skysail; in brief, he has not yet seen how narrow his world has been. Off the Grand Banks of Newfoundland—and after discovering that sailors are not quite delicate glass figures—Redburn again writes of Mr. Thompson, but on this occasion one detects a slight shift in attitude. The tendency to patronize is still evident, but in Redburn's voice is a suggestion of tolerance and perhaps respect. After noting that Mr. Thompson is a "serious old fellow, much given to metaphysics," he is incredulous to discover that the soiled book Thompson pores over every Sunday morning is the Bible. "I could hardly believe my eyes" (p. 81) is his shocked response. Evidently in Redburn's previous world blacks and Christianity were unassociated, Christianity being a religion for white civilized men and not for black bogeymen. Significantly, he assumes without question that his white mates, villainous as they show themselves to be, are on familiar terms with the church: ". . . I made bold to ask one of them, whether he was ever in the habit of going to church when he was ashore, or dropping in at the Floating Chapel I had seen lying off the dock in the East River at New York" (p. 48). That he should consider it probable for the white sailor to be a churchgoer and, at the same time, be shocked at the improbability of the black man with a Bible is indicative of Redburn's naive bias. After this discovery Redburn is, at least, less frightened of Thompson: "I loved to peep in upon him when he was thus absorbed" (p. 81) in reading the Bible. Though patronizing, he seems almost sympathetic: "Reading must have been very hard work for him; for he muttered to himself quite loud as he read" (p. 81). He describes Thompson's particular care of the cookhouse and even notes his pride in his status aboard ship: ". . . He had a warm love and affection for his cook-house. In fair weather, he spread the skirt of an old jacket before the door, by way of a mat; and screwed a small ringbolt into the door for a knocker; and wrote his name, 'Mr. Thompson,' over it, with a bit of red chalk" (p. 82). It is "Mister" Thompson, a title which, Redburn earlier observes, belongs to all officers, who "would take it for an insult if any seaman presumed to omit calling them so" (p. 39). Redburn, who earlier reacted with "dreadful loathing" to profanity, finds himself more able to tolerate Thompson's bad language, which grew especially pronounced when he tried to light his cooking fire during stormy weather: ". . . Under the circumstances, you could not blame him much, if he did rip a little, for it would have tried old Job's temper to be set to work making a fire in the water" (p. 82). He sees, too, that the cook is capable of moral judgments, once when Thompson condemns drunken captains and, again, when Thompson tries to reform the steward by holding up as an example the biblical Joseph.

Although Redburn's depiction of the cook indicates some recognition of the Negro as a man, it still retains the stock characteristics of the "stage" darky. As Baltimore was the "culinary high priest," Thompson is the "woolly Doctor of Divinity" (p. 137). His bow is one that "only a negro can make" (p. 305). Three Negro ministers who conduct a prayer meeting with Thompson are described as "a committee of three reverend-looking old darkies, who, besides their natural canonicals, wore quaker-cut black coats, and broad-brimmed black hats, and white neckcloths" (p. 82). After the prayer meeting in the cookhouse, "the congregation came out in a grand perspiration" (p. 82). Thompson also perspires: "Big drops of sweat would stand upon his brow, and roll off, till they hissed on the hot stove before him" (pp. 81–82). To Redburn only the blacks, never the white seamen, sweat. He still sees people in terms of myth: darkies are lazy and perspire with the least attempt at exertion. At this stage of his education into reality Redburn views the black man as a combination of human and stereotype; however, the comic elements, pronounced in the treatment of Baltimore and Annatoo, are faint here. At no time, for instance, is Thompson the butt of practical jokes, nor is his life an endless round of tribulations. In fact, he completes the cruise the wealthiest of the crew. As Redburn observes, Thompson's "piety proved profitable in restraining him from the expensive excesses of most seafaring men" (p. 305).

At the same time that Redburn "sees" the cook as something more than a scowling, unwashed darky, he offers his observations of the black steward Lavender. This "handsome, dandy mulatto" is another example of a dark-skinned character treated humorously in Melville's fiction. In part, the humor is of the "Mr. Bones" type and typifies a conventional image of the black as one given to flamboyancy and bright colors. Lavender sports "an uncommon head of frizzled hair, just like the large round brush used for washing windows." It is "well perfumed" and topped by a "gorgeous turban" (p. 83). His clothes are "all in the height of the exploded fashions, and of every kind of colour and cut. He had claret-coloured suits and snuff-coloured suits, and red velvet vests and buff and brimstone pantaloons, and several full suits of black, which, with his dark-coloured face, made him look quite clerical; like a serious young coloured gentleman of Barbados, about to take Orders" (p. 83). The ludicrous wardrobe is perfect for the end man. On his forefinger he wears "an uncommon large pursy ring . . . with something he called a real diamond in it; though it was very dim, and looked more like a glass eye than anything else" (p. 83). Lavender is a burlesque figure, a flashy Ham Bone, and, potentially, a comic foil to the "straight man" Thompson.

The mimicry, however, is not purely racial. Lavender is a roguish dandy at whose follies we would laugh whether he was white or black; whitewash him, and he could step on the

Restoration stage in the role of the sentimental fop: "He was a sentimental sort of a darky, and read the *Three Spaniards* and *Charlotte Temple,* and carried a lock of frizzled hair in his vest pocket, which he frequently volunteered to show to people, with his handkerchief to his eyes" (p. 83). Also, Lavender's response to Thompson cautioning him on his amorous indiscretions emphasizes not the stereotype darky but the sentimental rogue:

And Lavender would look serious, and say that he knew it was all true—he was a wicked youth, he knew it—he had broken a good many hearts, and many eyes were weeping for him even then. . . . But how could he help it? He hadn't made his handsome face, and fine head of hair, and graceful figure. It was not *he,* but the others, that were to blame; for his bewitching person turned all heads and subdued all hearts, wherever he went. And then he would look very serious and penitent, and go up to the little glass, and pass his hands through his hair, and see how his whiskers were coming on. [Pp. 83–84]

Except for the absence of verbal swordplay (with most of the hits striking the dandy), Lavender is an American Sir Fopling Flutter. With Redburn, the reader smiles not at Lavender's "Negro" traits but at his "human" folly—for the same reason that one smiles at a white dandy, Lieutenant Selvagee in Melville's next work, *White-Jacket.* Selvagee possesses "all the intrepid effeminacy of your true dandy," takes "cologne-water baths," and sports "lace-bordered handkerchiefs." There is, significantly enough, "no getting the lavender out of" Selvagee.[3] *White-Jacket* offers other samples of sea dandies who, though white, are type-cast as Lavender is. These "silk-sock-gentry" spend most of their time "reading novels and romances; talking over their love affairs ashore; and comparing notes concerning the melancholy and sentimental career which drove them—poor young gentlemen—into the hardhearted Navy."[4] Like Lavender, they take pride in "pluming themselves upon the cut of their trowsers and the glossiness of their tarpaulins."[5] Lavender, then, is a type—partly the stereotype darky but, more so, a human type—and, skin color notwithstanding, he enjoys the same fictional status as do the dandies of *White-Jacket.*

Thus far, Redburn's impressions, though they admit of a growing awareness, particularly in his attitude toward Mr. Thompson, still emanate from a mind shaped by the conventions of a "discreet life." But Redburn's education continues; as Mason notes, "The further that Redburn sails from his old home into new experience, the less does Melville recur to farcical incident, and the surer is his capacity to observe and transmit impressions."[6] The experiences which produce this capacity to "observe" and, it must be added, to feel, are many: his romantic enthusiasm for the sea is eroded by the lashings of the North Atlantic and the harsh discipline of the ship; his naive view of the world is marred by the searing recognition of evil, most appalling in the person of a shipmate, the malignant Jackson, and shocking in the unmentionably sordid vices rampant in Liverpool; the hideous social evils bred by poverty and man's indifference to human misery wrench him from his self-centered world. The condescending pity of the adolescent is replaced by the genuine compassion of the adult. In short, Redburn begins to confront life stripped of the local and social conventions which blurred his earlier observations. Little irony remains in Melville's portrayal of Redburn; instead, there emerges a narrator purged of his egotism and romanticism, speaking from a position of involvement and identification with others. Hence, his attitude toward the nonwhites now begins to be different from his earlier responses to Thompson and Lavender.

Sights of poverty "in almost endless vistas" in the miserable streets of Liverpool bring to Redburn a startling revelation—"the absence of negroes; who in the large towns in the 'free states' of America, almost always form a considerable portion of the destitute" (pp. 201–02). This linking of the Negro with want indicates, in some measure, how Redburn has replaced self-pity with recognition of a social ill in his own land. He is also led to observe, "In Liverpool . . . the negro steps with a prouder pace, and lifts his head like a man; for here, no such exaggerated feeling exists in respect to him as in America" (p. 202). Such an admission under-

scores the "exaggerated feeling" which colored his own earlier views of Thompson and Lavender and again reflects his
growing social consciousness. Most significant is Redburn's
response to seeing Lavender and a "good-looking English
woman" walking arm in arm down the streets of Liverpool.
In this instance, Lavender is "dressed very handsomely," and
his "stock" characteristics are not mentioned. "In New York,"
Redburn reflects, "such a couple would have been mobbed in
three minutes; and the steward would have been lucky to
escape with whole limbs" (p. 202). Here he confesses his
earlier misconceptions, saying that his surprise at the treatment of the colored was occasioned by his youth, inexperi-
ence, and "local and social prejudices." He then utters an
appropriate testimony to his newly-acquired vision: ". . . A
little reflection showed that, after all, it was but recognizing
his [the Negro's] claims to humanity and normal equality; so
that, in some things, we Americans leave to other countries
the carrying out of the principle that stands at the head of
our Declaration of Independence" (p. 202). Redburn has
come a considerable distance from the naive adolescent who
was shocked at the sight of a Negro reading the Bible. As
Sedgwick observes, "He has shaken off 'those local and social
prejudices that are the marring of most men, and from which,
for the mass, there seems no possible escape,' and to which,
it would seem, Americans are peculiarly subject."[7] Through
the development of Redburn's growth to wisdom and compassion, Melville could be indicating how in the ideal society
the nonwhite should be regarded. The foolish, the selfish, the
uninitiated categorize the nonwhite in accord with the role
society assigns him, as either an inferior buffoon or a scowling
savage; the humane and the wise see him as a human and an
equal. Near the end of his narrative, in a tone that recalls the
defense of the Polynesians in *Typee* and *Omoo* and the impassioned outrage at slavery in *Mardi,* Redburn indicts the
Christian world; in so doing he stands a man, no longer
childishly provincial and self-centered:

We talk of the Turks, and abhor the cannibals; but may not some of *them* go to heaven before some of *us*? We may have civilized bodies and yet barbarous souls. We are blind to the real sights of this world; deaf to its voice; and dead to its death. And not till we know that one grief outweighs ten thousand joys will become what Christianity is striving to make us. [P. 292]

Redburn's recognition of the myriad griefs and indignities characterizing life in Liverpool also leads him to a new awareness of another human evil—the African slave trade. At the base of Admiral Nelson's statue are four figures "in various attitudes of humiliation and despair." These figures are emblematic of Nelson's victories, but Redburn "never could look at their swarthy limbs and manacles without being involuntarily reminded of four American slaves in the marketplace." To him, they are "woe-begone" figures. One bows his head "as if he had given up hope"; another buries his head "in despondency" (p. 155). Considering Redburn's initial response to the "woolly Doctor of Divinity," one must again be impressed with the changes which this young voyager has undergone. The sight of the "bronze captives" also reminds Redburn that the African slave trade was once the life's blood of Liverpool commerce and that the abolition movement had occasioned considerable controversy in the city. This controversy Redburn terms "the struggle between sordid interest and humanity" (p. 156). He also praises the abolition activities of "the intrepid enemy of the trade," Roscoe: this "good and great" man "exerted his fine talents" toward the suppression of the trade and "had no small share in the triumph of sound policy and humanity" (p. 156). Again, the concern evidenced here by the emphasis on the African's claim to "humanity" is that of a young man's developing consciousness of the interrelationship of all men. It is this consciousness which leads Redburn to remark, ". . . There is a touch of divinity even in brutes" (p. 197), an observation that recalls the slave in *Mardi*, who, though considered a "brute," envisions himself an angel. With this consciousness comes an optimistic prophecy for America: "On this Western Hemisphere all tribes and people are forming into one federated whole; and there is a future which shall see the estranged children of Adam restored as to the old hearthstone in Eden" (p. 169).

Although race is not a major concern in *Redburn*, the book does offer insights into Melville's racial attitudes and, to a considerable degree, echoes and extends his responses to the nonwhite evident in his first three works. Like *Mardi*, it reflects repugnance and pity toward bondage and toward the oppressed; as in the first three works, it portrays the nonwhites in a dual light, partly with sympathy and humor and partly with tolerance and respect; it reinforces an important focus of *Typee, Omoo*, and *Mardi*: a recognition of the nonwhite's claim to humanity.

5. WHITE-JACKET

Nor . . . is the general ignorance or depravity of any race of men to be alleged as an apology for tyranny over them. On the contrary, it cannot admit of a reasonable doubt, in any unbiased mind conversant with the interior of a man-of-war, that most of the sailor inequities practiced therein are indirectly to be ascribed to the morally debasing effects of the unjust, despotic, and degrading laws under which the man-of-war's man lives.

"As a man-of-war that sails through the sea, so this earth that sails through the air. We mortals are all on board a fast-sailing, never-sinking world-frigate, of which God was the shipwright; and she is but one craft in a Milky-Way fleet, of which God is the Lord High Admiral."[1] So Melville begins the final chapter of this fifth work, *White-Jacket*. The analogy of the vessel *Neversink* to the earth echoes the book's subtitle, *The World in a Man-of-War*, and emphasizes the duality of its discourse. This account of Melville's last voyage, as an enlisted seaman aboard the frigate *United States* homeward bound from the Pacific, is more than just chronicle, for its narrator directly and indirectly parallels events and people aboard ship with events and people aboard the world. This narrator, seaman White-Jacket, like the matured Redburn is sensitive to and repelled by the indignities to which man subjects his fellows. More than Redburn, however, White-Jacket sees these indignities in larger contexts than a single ship. The abuses he attacks are the abuses of the world. *White-Jacket,* says Ronald Mason, is "the fulfillment of the apprenticeship and education of Melville the sailor."[2] It is, in addition, an "education" which crystallizes the social ideas of the narrator so that he speaks, not from the self-centered viewpoint of the unformed adolescent, but, as Hennig Cohen indicates, "from the position of a commitment to American democratic brotherhood, a respect for the rights of the individual, and a sense of Christian charity."[3] In essence, then, White-Jacket's concern for humanity is built on the attitudes that Redburn begins to embrace, particularly the latter's observation "that one grief outweighs ten thousand joys."

The crew of the world-frigate includes several blacks. The narrator's description of and attitude toward these characters reflect, to a degree, the dual response to the nonwhite characters in Melville's previous works. Again, the marks of the stereotype are readily apparent; more pronounced, however, is the attitude of respect accorded to some of the nonwhites, an attitude consistent with the humanitarian tone which pervades the entire book. In addition to his observations of the blacks, White-Jacket's outraged response to the "lash" is of some aid in determining Melville's racial attitudes. Specifically, White-Jacket attacks flogging in the United States Navy; but if the *Neversink* is the world, the logical worldly parallel to flogging is the scourging of slaves. As Cohen observes, ". . . In the political order of the *Neversink,* seamen have much in common with slaves in their position at the bottom of the hierarchy and their subjection to the whip."[4] If this extension of the analogy seems strained, one needs only to recall how dominant a part the lash occupies in the discussion of slavery in *Mardi.* Witness the slave in Vivenza whose striped back corresponds to the flag, or the other thrall who— under the lash—acknowledges himself a brute. Leon Howard is representative of those critics who attach to Melville's handing of flogging in *White-Jacket* a significance which makes the act considerably more than a naval abuse: "A flogging

conducted with all the formality of institutionalized civilization became his [Melville's] symbol of all the indignity that
man could heap on man, and that symbol was to dance before
his eyes during his entire term of naval service and remain
vividly in his memory for many years thereafter."[5] In short,
then, both the continued respect accorded to black characters and the indictment of flogging amplify the racial observations evident in Melville's first four books.

The blacks who appear in White-Jacket are cast in part as
humorous stereotypes stamped with the stock characteristics
of Baltimore and Lavender. Their comic intent is evident in
the names of four of them: Old Coffee, a reflection on either
his color or his culinary art, Sunshine, Rose-Water, and May
Day—"poetical appellations" suggesting the dramatis per-
sonae of a minstrel show and possibly alluding to the Negro's
supposed bright, carefree manner and his fondness for aro-
matic cosmetics. The last three are, typically, "jolly Africans"
who obediently "spring" to their tasks of polishing the cooking
kettles and throw themselves into a "violent perspiration," all
the while singing as they work, "thus making gleeful their toil
by their cheering songs" (p. 58). Sunshine, instead of merely
complaining, as do the white seamen, about the stoppage of
the daily grog ration, "blubbers" in Jim Crow fashion, "No
grog on de day dat tried men's souls!" (p. 90). Rose-Water,
"a slender and rather handsome mulatto," is, as his name
suggests, Lavender moved from the *Highlander* to the *Neversink*. His reading tastes are of an "elegant nature, as evidenced
by his exalted opinion of the literary merits of the *Loves of
the Angels*," a work he calls *"de charmingest of wolumes"*
(pp. 168–69). The dominant impression created by these
touches is that of a formula rather than of human beings, for
the emphasis falls on certain assumptions about the Negro
character—his happy-go-lucky spirit, his spit-and-polish ab-
sorption in menial tasks, his quickness both to perspire and to
sing. Each confirms Walter I. Lewis's estimate of the Negro
as having "a laughing soul that places a bouquet of joy and
sunshine where the somber draping of woe would so often be
found."[6]

Old Coffee, too, is a source of some humor; and, as was
the case with the cooks Baltimore and Mr. Thompson, the
humor is characterized by a tone of mock grandeur. True,
White-Jacket refers to Old Coffee as "a dignified coloured
gentleman," but he also designates him as "a high and
mighty functionary" (p. 58), a title echoing "the culinary
high priest" (Baltimore) and the "woolly Doctor of Divinity"
(Mr. Thompson). In describing the naval ritual in which the
cook presents the daily mess to the deck officer, White-Jacket
depicts both the occasion and the cook with mock solemnity:

Nor was Old Coffee at all blind to the dignity and importance of
the ceremony, in which he enacted so conspicuous a part. He
preserved the utmost rectitude of carriage; and when it was "Duff
Day," he would advance with his tin truncheon borne high aloft,
exhibiting a pale, round duff surmounting the blood-red mass of
beef:—he looked something like the figure in the old painting of
the executioner presenting the head of St. John the Baptist in a
charger. [Pp. 285–86]

Although he is not subjected to an endless round of practical
jokes, Old Coffee is apparently easy to bribe and to dupe,
as evidenced by this slapstick scene:

Now the only way that a sailor, after preparing his *dunderfunk*
[hard biscuit, hashed and mixed with beef fat, molasses and
water], could get it cooked on board the *Neversink,* was by slily
going to *Old Coffee* . . . and bribing him to put it into his oven.
And as some such dishes or other are all well known to be all
the time in the oven, a set of unprincipled gourmands are constantly on the lookout for the chance of stealing them. Generally,
two or three league together, and while one engages Old Coffee
in some interesting conversation touching his wife and family at
home, another snatches the first thing he can lay hands on in the
oven, and rapidly passes it to the third man, who at his earliest
leisure disappears with it. [Pp. 132–33]

With a banjo or two and a bright scarf to accent their naval
garb, Old Coffee and his assistants would be choice candi-
dates for a nautical minstrel show.

The stereotype, however, is not the complete picture.
White-Jacket, like Redburn, acknowledges the blacks' claim
to humanity; in fact, he goes beyond mere recognition of

them as men to regard them with both admiration and genuine compassion. Rose-Water may at first be the object of White-Jacket's smiles, but when he must bare his back to the lash, the humor is gone. In the chapter entitled "Fun in a Man-of-War," White-Jacket briefly summarizes the physically punishing "games" occasionally permitted the sailors, but he is not so brief in his account of *head-bumping,* a brutal sport in which Rose-Water is forced to be a prime contender. This "sport," Captain Claret's "especial favorite," is reserved for Negroes, who butt at each other "like rams." "Whites will not answer," for Captain Claret; in his mind, the hard head and the brute instinct are integral parts of the Negro make-up. Rose-Water abhors Claret's pastime primarily because his opponent is the captain's favorite, the "bull-negro" May Day, whose skull is "like an iron tea-kettle." Yet he must obey his captain and defend himself against being butted into the ocean. Here White-Jacket's compassion and anger are reminiscent of the travelers' response in *Mardi* to the oppressed in the extreme south of Vivenza: "I used to pity poor Rose-Water from the bottom of my heart. But my pity was almost aroused into indignation at a sad sequel to one of these gladiatorial scenes" (p. 275). That sequel is instigated by May Day's calling his opponent a "nigger." Insulted, Rose-Water cites his parentage with pride: "... His mother, a black slave, had been one of the mistresses of a Virginia planter belonging to one of the oldest families in that state." White-Jacket neither condemns nor condones the miscegenation except to call the mulatto's remark an "innocent disclosure" (p. 275). At any rate, the insults culminate in a fight, an offense for which the punishment is twelve lashes. Claret, who relished the "sporting" encounter of his two "rams," pronounces sentence: "I'll teach you two men that, though I now and then permit you to *play,* I will have no *fighting*" (p. 276). Claret's double standard leads White-Jacket to an impassioned outburst at the vicissitudes of captains—and of slaveholders: "How can they have the heart? Methinks, if but once I smiled upon a man—never mind how much beneath me—I could not bring myself to condemn him to the shocking misery of the lash. . . . Of all insults, the temporary condescension of a master to a slave is the most outrageous and galling" (p. 276). Turning to the degraded Rose-Water, White-Jacket utters one of the most revealing remarks on race in all of Melville's works:

Poor mulatto! . . . one of an oppressed race, they degrade you like a hound. Thank God! I am white. Yet I had seen whites also scourged; for, black or white, all my shipmates were liable to that. Still, there is something in us, somehow, that, in the most degraded condition, we snatch at a chance to deceive ourselves into a fancied superiority to others, whom we suppose lower in the scale than ourselves.
    Poor Rose-Water! . . . poor mulatto! Heaven send you a release from your humiliation! [P. 277]

White-Jacket's bitterness toward those who see the blacks as brutish performers, his unconcealed pity for a member of an "oppressed race," his admission of self-deception regarding "fancied superiority to others"—all constitute a fervent belief in a democracy which venerates the special value of all human beings.

Whether or not the flogging of Rose-Water is a dramatic turning point in White-Jacket's racial attitudes is difficult to say; it is noteworthy, however, that the blacks who appear after the flogging scene are treated with respect and admiration. The stock characteristics are replaced by human traits. The result once again points to a dual response on Melville's part toward the nonwhite.

In this connection, two blacks aboard the *Neversink,* both introduced after Rose-Water's flogging, deserve considerable consideration. The first of these blacks is Tawny, "a staid and sober seaman, very intelligent, with a fine, frank bearing, one of the best men in the ship, and held in high estimation by everyone" (p. 311). Such praise and respect is accorded only two other characters, the most admirable in the book, the noble Ushant and the magnificent Jack Chase. Tawny is a special favorite of the main-top men and on tranquil nights is invited up to discourse on his experiences.

Impressed out of a New England merchantman and forced into service aboard the English frigate the *Macedonian,* he found "It was a most bitter thing to lift their hands against the flag of that country which harbored the mothers that bore them" (p. 312). As the *Macedonian* prepared to engage the *Neversink,* Tawny and his impressed countrymen begged the English captain "to release them from their guns, and allow them to remain neutral during the conflict." To no avail; under penalty of being shot on the spot, "side by side with their country's foes, Tawny and his companions toiled at the guns" (p. 312). The victory fell to the American man-of-war partly because of superior firepower, partly because some of the English guns had been "spiked," i.e., rendered useless. The impressed Americans did serve their flag. Tawny, a "truth-telling man," would also escort White-Jacket along the main-deck batteries, pointing out battle scars and telling of "beams and carlines . . . spattered with blood and brains" and "bits of human flesh sticking in the ringbolts" (p. 316). These and other details of the great battle between the *Macedonian* and the *Neversink* he relates soberly without glorifying the great god of battle. It is quite possible that Tawny is partly responsible for White-Jacket's pacifism. As White-Jacket puts it, "Tawny's recitals were enough to snap this man-of-war world's sword in its scabbard" (p. 316). In no way does Tawny appear in a derogatory light. The impression he creates is that of a wise, highly respected man.

Another black introduced by White-Jacket is Guinea, a Virginian slave, whose wages are paid to his owner, the purser. "Sleek and round, his ebon face fairly polished with content; ever gay and hilarious; ever ready to laugh and joke" (p. 379), Guinea appears equipped with the stock features which would place him with the stereotypes of the kitchen; however, he has a more significant function—ironically, this bond slave is the envy of the wage slaves. "Never," says White-Jacket, "did I feel my condition as a man-of-war's man so keenly as when seeing this Guinea freely circulating about the decks in citizen's clothes, and, through the influence of his master, almost entirely exempted from the disciplinary degradation of the Caucasian crew" (p. 379). An incident dramatizing the ironic freedom of Guinea is worth citing in full:

One morning, when all hands were called to witness punishment, the Purser's slave, as usual, was observed to be hurrying down the ladders toward the ward-room, his face wearing that peculiar pinched blueness, which, in the negro, answers to the paleness caused by nervous agitation in the white. "Where are you going, Guinea?" cried the deck-officer, a humorous gentleman, who sometimes diverted himself with the purser's slave, and well knew what answer he would now receive from him. "Where are you going, Guinea?" said this officer; "turn about; don't you hear the call, sir?" " 'Scuse me, massa!" said the slave, with a low salutation; "I can't 'tand it; I can't, indeed, massa!" and, so saying, he disappeared beyond the hatchway. He was the only person on board, except the hospital-steward and the invalids of the sickbay, who was exempted from being present at the administering of the scourge. Accustomed to light and easy duties from his birth, and so fortunate as to meet with none but gentle masters, Guinea, though a bondman, liable to be saddled with a mortgage, like a horse—Guinea, in india-rubber manacles, enjoyed the liberties of the world. [P. 379]

The incident tells much. First, unlike the seamen who envy Guinea, the deck-officer obviously regards the slave as an amusing diversion, the equivalent of Captain Claret's "headbumping" game. Second and more significant is the anguished distaste registered by Guinea. The servile dialect notwithstanding, his remarks reveal an emotional revulsion equal to that of White-Jacket himself. Although "a bondman, liable to be saddled with a mortgage, like a horse," Guinea feels; he is no formula.

Also of considerable interest is White-Jacket's approval of Guinea's owner:

Though his body-and-soul proprietor, the Purser never in any way individualized me while I served on board the frigate, and never did me a good office of any kind (it was hardly in his power), yet, from his pleasant, kind, indulgent manner toward his slave, I always imputed to him a generous heart, and cherished an involuntary friendliness toward him. Upon our arrival home, his treatment of Guinea, under circumstances peculiarly calculated to stir up the resentment of a slave-owner, still more augmented my estimation of the Purser's good heart. [P. 379]

There exists then such a thing as a "good" slaveowner, who, in contrast with the heartless overseer of *Mardi,* replaces the lash with kindness. The "circumstances" alluded to at the end of the above passage revolve around the suit of some abolitionists to secure Guinea's freedom. The reformers are not concerned with Guinea's opinion of his fate. Critic Charles Anderson, in relating the actual court case involving Guinea (Robert Lucas) and his owner, observes, "Here was an instance of a kind master deprived of a contented slave by the intermeddling of Abolitionists; and Melville, himself a reformer, was the one to throw this denial of the good effects of their philanthropy in their face."[7] It would be difficult to quarrel with this conclusion. White-Jacket is an abolitionist only in his wish to see men respect the essential manliness of their fellow beings. Admittedly, such a condition may seem impossible within the framework of a system in which men may own other men, but it appears to be White-Jacket's position.

On the basis of this incident alone, one could conclude that White-Jacket deems slavery an evil only so far as it fosters tyranny and brutality. Such a conclusion, however, would exclude another possible reason for White-Jacket's favorable view of the slaveowner. Melville could be condemning through White-Jacket those dedicated "reformers" who zealously uphold a principle regarding man but who disregard the real man.[8] Conceivably, White-Jacket is not inconsistently condoning slavery so much as he is indicting the "do-gooders" who, in promoting their cause, are oblivious to the slave's feelings. Whether Guinea wishes to be free or to remain under the indulgent care of the purser is irrelevant to the abolitionists. The contrast is keen—the "good heart" of the purser makes possible a relationship marked by generosity and kindness; the theorizing minds of the philanthropists ignore the human element. Melville echoes this position on the abolition movement in the words of the herb-doctor in *The Confidence-Man*. Accused of being an abolitionist, the herb-doctor replies, "If by abolitionist you mean a zealot, I am none; but if you mean a man, who being a man, feels for all men, slaves included, and by any lawful act, opposed to nobody's interest, and therefore rousing nobody's enmity, would willingly abolish suffering . . . from among mankind, irrespective of colour, then am I what you say."[9] Little wonder, then, that White-Jacket speaks kindly of the slaveowner. As for Guinea, he is not a servile, happy-go-lucky darky, not an object of humor, except to the deck-officer. He is a man whose sensitivity is respected both by his owner and by White-Jacket.

As already mentioned, White-Jacket devotes much of his record of the "World in a Man-of-War" to a vehement denunciation of flogging in the United States Navy; and, as discussed earlier, there is in Melville a strong association of the lash with the African slave. It is a symbol of oppression, and in the world analogous to the *Neversink* the back on which the lash is most frequently laid is black.

One of the most revealing observations of White-Jacket is his justification of rebellion against oppression: ". . . Every American man-of-war's man would be morally justified in resisting the scourge to the uttermost; and, in so resisting, would be religiously justified in what would be judicially styled 'the act of mutiny' itself" (p. 145). Read "African slave" instead of "American man-of-war's man." The result would be a reinforcement of Yoomy's declaration in *Mardi*: " 'Tis right to fight for freedom, whoever be the thrall." Elaborating on his justification of "mutiny," White-Jacket indicts the scourge as "opposed to the essential dignity of man" and "utterly repugnant to the spirit of our democratic institutions; indeed . . . it involves a lingering trait of the worst times of a barbarous feudal aristocracy" (p. 146). In an impassioned plea for its abolition, he argues:

No matter, then, what may be the consequences of its abolition; no matter if we have to dismantle our fleets, and our unprotected commerce should fall a prey to the spoiler, the awful admonitions of justice and humanity demand that abolition without procrastination; in a voice that is not to be mistaken, demand that abolition to-day. It is not a dollar-and-cent question of expediency; it is a matter of right and wrong. And if any man can lay his hand on his heart, and solemnly say that this scourging is right, let that man but once feel the lash on his own back, and in his agony you will hear the apostate call the seventh heavens to witness that it is wrong. And, in the name of immortal manhood, would to God that every man who upholds this thing were scourged at the gangway till he recanted. [P. 146]

Above all, flogging causes loss of "manhood" in its humiliating barrage against a man's dignity. White-Jacket does admit exceptions: "Yet so untouchable is true dignity, that there are cases wherein to be flogged at the gangway is no dishonor" (p. 142). The most dramatic example in the book is the noble Ushant, who, after being flogged for retaining his beard—"the token of manhood"—declares to the master-at-arms, ". . . 'Tis no dishonor when he who would dishonor you only dishonors himself" (p. 366). In essence, to retain the "essential dignity of man, which no legislator has a right to violate" (p. 146), to keep inviolate the "image of his [man's] Creator" (p. 142), the oppressed are justified in defying degradation. Such defiance is dramatically realized in White-Jacket's emotional turmoil when he himself is brought to the mast for punishment. Wrongfully accused, his pleas of innocence "thrown in his teeth," White-Jacket finds that his only alternative to degradation is an instinctive turn to violence:

My blood seemed clotting in my veins; I felt icy cold at the tip of my fingers, and a dimness was before my eyes. But through that dimness the boatswain's mate, scourge in hand, loomed like a giant, and Captain Claret, and the blue sea seen through the opening at the gangway, showed with an awful vividness. I cannot analyze my heart, though it then stood still within me. But the thing that swayed me to my purpose was not altogether the thought that Captain Claret was about to degrade me, and that I had taken an oath with my soul that he should not. No, I felt my man's manhood so bottomless within me, that no word, no blow, no scourge of Captain Claret could cut me deep enough for that. I but swung to an instinct in me—the instinct diffused through all animated nature, the same that prompts even a worm to turn under the heel. Locking souls with him, I meant to drag Captain Claret from this earthly tribunal of his to that of Jehovah, and let Him decide between us. No other way could I escape the scourge. [P. 280]

Several parallels to *Mardi* are evident here. Again, the emphasis is on the preservation of "manhood"; unlike the slaves in *Mardi,* who "unmanned . . . know not what they are," White-Jacket asserts his identity as a human being. Also, as in *Mardi,* the rebellion will be judged by Jehovah. (Yoomy declares, "Oro [God] will van the right." Babbalanja, too, associates "judgment" with "retribution.") To White-Jacket, retribution is an inalienable privilege and, as in *Mardi,* a last resort:

Nature has not implanted any power in man that was not meant to be exercised at times, though too often our powers have been abused. The privilege, inborn and inalienable, that every man has, of dying himself, and inflicting death upon another, was not given to us without a purpose. These are the last resources of an insulted and unendurable existence. [P. 280]

The entire episode, though considered purely fictional by most critics, is indicative of Melville's empathy with the oppressed and his indignation toward the oppressor.

Underscoring the value placed on "manhood" is the attitude of the officers toward any sailor who shows "some dignity within"—traits of "manly freedom." Such a seaman is as "unendurable, as an erect, lofty-minded African would be to some slave-driving planter" (p. 385). Instead, the officers (and, by implication, "slave-driving planter[s]") prefer a creature like seaman Landless, who "danced quite as often at the gangway, under the lash, as in the sailor dance-houses ashore," yet responded to these repeated humiliations with "indifference" (p. 384). White-Jacket's estimate of Landless speaks for itself: he is "a fellow without shame, without a soul, so dead to the least dignity of manhood that he could hardly be called a man" (p. 384).

Finally, to the overseers of the world who see the tribe of Hamo as "soulless pointers" and who justify enslavement on the grounds of caring for an inferior race, White-Jacket offers a rebuttal: "Nor . . . is the general ignorance or depravity of any race of men to be alleged as an apology for tyranny over them" (p. 304). This observation anticipates Ishmael's remark in *Moby-Dick*: ". . . Be a man's intellectual superiority what it will, it can never assume the practical, available supremacy over other men, without the aid of some sort of external acts and entrenchments, always, in themselves, more or less paltry and base" (VII, 182). In Vivenza and on the *Neversink,* that "base," "external" aid is the lash.

In *White-Jacket* Melville is not concerned with the question of whether the dark skin encases a man or a devil. For the most part, the blacks and browns are, though occasionally humorous, respected as men. As men, whites and darks alike are "images" of God; to enslave, to brutalize them is to deny their fundamental equality, their "manliness." Any system, whether the United States Navy in *White-Jacket* or slavery in *Mardi,* which fosters brutality, which strips man of his dignity, must expect retribution. As White-Jacket himself declares: "Indifferent as to who may be the parties concerned, I but desire to see wrong things righted and equal justice administered to all" (p. 304).

6. *MOBY-DICK*

> *No school like a ship for studying human nature.*
>
> —*Taji*

> *...A whale ship was my Yale College and my Harvard.*
>
> —*Ishmael*

The images of the nonwhite reflected in *Typee, Omoo, Mardi, Redburn,* and *White-Jacket,* present complexities and contradictions not easily reconciled in any kind of bare description or analysis. The variety of roles, some of which overlap, fall generally into four categories: olive-skinned Polynesians, magnificent physical specimens primarily virtuous and humane but easily moved to hostility; South Sea savages prone to ferocious vindictiveness; stock "darkies," objects of laughter and abuse; natives and Negroes humanized by their sense of pride and self-respect. Here is a variety of roles which could be assigned to any cast of characters, regardless of skin color. On this basis alone, one senses a high level of tolerance on Melville's part. Further, if one considers that the comic patronizing (i.e., in the case of the "darkies") is marked by sympathy and good-natured affection and that the savage vindictiveness is usually provoked, one is left with those characters who in their sense of common humanity evoke both tolerance and admiration. As Melville stands on

81

the threshold of *Moby-Dick*, his first five works demonstrate a consistent respect for man's instinctive sense of his own dignity and an insistence on the inviolability of man's personality. In the year of *Mardi* and *White-Jacket*, Melville states as much in his review of Parkman's *Oregon Trail*: ". . . Wherever we recognize the image of God, let us reverence it though it hung from the gallows."[1] Thus, "sprung from one head, and made in one image,"[2] men have a basic claim to equality. Such an affirmation of democratic and humanistic ideals is not mere rhetoric; as the previous chapters of this study have demonstrated, these ideals are confirmed in Tommo's admiration of the Marquesans, in his repugnance toward the white despoilers of Tahitian culture and morality, in the anger and pity evoked by the plight of the tribe of Hamo, in Redburn's recognition of the Negro's claim to humanity, and in White-Jacket's acknowledgment of man, white or black, as an "image" of God.

In essence, a belief in human equality based on "that immaculate manliness we feel within ourselves, so far within us, that it remains intact though all the outer character seem gone"[3] appears central to Melville's social philosophy. That belief echoes and reechoes in his masterpiece *Moby-Dick*, a book celebrating the dignity of man—the dignity "shining in the arm what wields a pick or drives a spike; that democratic dignity which, on all hands, radiates from God, Himself! The great God absolute! The centre and circumference of all democracy! His omnipresence, our divine equality!" (VII, 144). At first glance, to claim a "dignity" for the *Pequod's* crew of renegades, savages, and castoffs, all dedicated to the hellish pursuit of their captain's vengeance, would appear to be nonsense. Ishmael's invocation to God, however, reminds us that God's image, man, "though it hung from the gallows," is deserving of respect:

If, then, to meanest mariners, and renegades and castaways, I shall hereafter ascribe high qualities, though dark; weave round them tragic graces; if even the most mournful, perchance the most abused, among them all, shall at times lift himself to the exalted

mounts; if I shall touch that workman's arm with some ethereal
light; if I shall spread a rainbow over his disastrous set of sun;
then against all mortal critics bear me out in it, thou just Spirit
of Equality, which hast spread one royal mantle of humanity over
all my kind! Bear me out in it, thou great democratic God! who
didst not refuse to the swart convict, Bunyan, the pale, poetic
pearl; Thou who didst clothe with doubly hammered leaves of
finest gold, the stumped and paupered arm of old Cervantes;
Thou who didst pick up Andrew Jackson from the pebbles; who
didst hurl him upon a war-horse; who didst thunder him higher
than a throne! Thou who, in all Thy mighty, earthly marchings,
ever cullest Thy selectest champions from the kingly commons;
bear me out in it, O God! [VII, 144]

Ishmael's plea is apparently answered, for on the deck of the
Pequod "champions from the kingly commons"—champions
whose skins are dark as well as white—dramatize the necessity of acknowledging what Ishmael calls the "common continent of men" (VII, 149). *Moby-Dick* demonstrates forcefully
and glowingly Herman Melville's freedom from racial prejudice.

The quest for Moby-Dick is survived by a single member
of the *Pequod's* crew—Ishmael, a solitary voice left to tell the
tale of Captain Ahab and the great white whale. He is a
meditative man, a Melville, given to probing the problem of
the universe and the interrelationships of its creatures.
Throughout his narrative, Ishmael seeks to understand, to
comprehend not just the whale but the "Anacharsis Clootz
deputation from all the isles of the sea, and all the ends of
the earth, accompanying Old Ahab in the *Pequod*"[4] (VII,
149). His vow to assign "high" as well as "dark" qualities to
the crew is, like his passion to pursue every detail of Leviathan, an earnest attempt to reduce the foreign and the unknown to intelligibility.

From the start, Ishmael is alert to the dangers of severance
from the human family. He stands, himself, on the brink of
total isolation. His is a "splintered heart," his a "maddened
hand" turned against a world he calls "wolfish" (VII, 62).
"Grim about the mouth" and "a damp, drizzly November" in
his soul, he must fight off the compulsion to step into the

streets and knock off people's hats. Ishmael then turns to the sea, his "substitute for pistol and ball" (VII, 1). To confine his motives to escapism, however, is to ignore the distinct possibility that he is seeking in the sea a redefinition of himself. Such a motive is evident in his explanation of the attraction the sea holds for landsmen and, presumably, for himself:

But look! here come more crowds, pacing straight for the water, and seemingly bound for a dive. Strange! Nothing will content them but the extremest limit of the land; loitering under the shady lee of yonder warehouses will not suffice. No. They must get just as nigh the water as they possibly can without falling in. And there they stand—miles of them—leagues. Inlanders all, they come from lanes and alleys, streets and avenues—north, east, south, and west. Yet here they all unite. [VII, 2]

Harry Levin has noted that "Melville, like Joseph Conrad, acknowledged 'the bond of the sea,' regarding all men who loved the sea as brothers."[5] Ishmael, too, views the sea as a unifying force and, perhaps, as a means of making whole his "splintered heart" by reuniting him with his fellow "inlanders." Repeatedly, the observant Ishmael notes the insular nature of landsmen and also seems vaguely aware of the dangers inherent in such a state. About Captain Peleg, part owner of the *Pequod,* he says, "I saw that . . . this old seaman, as an insulated Quakerish Nantucketer, was full of his insular prejudices, and rather distrustful of all aliens, unless they hailed from Cape Cod or the Vineyard" (VII, 88). As for the inhabitants of Nantucket, they "retain in an uncommon measure the peculiarities of the Quaker, only variously and anomalously modified by things altogether alien and heterogeneous" (VII, 91). No Quaker or Nantucketer, Ishmael is still an islander, and he must "go awhaling," for, as he says, ". . . Islanders seem to make the best whalemen" (VII, 149). The vessel on which he sails carries a crew of islanders. Ishmael calls them "Isolatoes . . . not acknowledging the common continent of men, but each Isolato living on a separate continent of his own" (VII, 149). Like Whitman's spider isolated on a promontory but seeking to "catch somewhere," Ishmael, evincing a consciousness of man's lonely soul and seeking to merge himself with something or someone, goes to sea—where all men "unite."

"Unite" they do, for aboard the *Pequod,* Ishmael notes early that the Isolatoes are "federated along one keel" (VII, 149). Significantly, the federation of men includes Negroes, South Sea savages, American Indians, and Orientals. Ishmael's experiences with and observations of these nonwhites bring him to an affirmation of the words of *Mardi's* narrator: ". . . the natives and families, flocks and folds on the earth; one and all, brothers in essence—oh, be we brothers indeed!" (p. 12).

This sense of brotherhood is a dominant theme of *Moby-Dick;* it is founded not on any Emersonian theory but on a profound respect for individual man irrespective of skin color. Further, this respect is acquired through experience with and close observation of the nonwhite members of the *Pequod's* "federation." One can hardly disagree with Howard Vincent, who, in seeing Ishmael's democratic faith as Melville's, observes, "To have achieved a faith like Melville's while fully conscious, as he was, of man's misery, his meanness, his fallen estate betokens not a bland superficial optimism, but a profound love of life—what Keats called the 'love of good and ill.' "[6] One might add that it betokens an acceptance of the dark-skinned races as essential equals—"that common decency of recognition which is the meanest slave's right" (VII, 309–10).

Starbuck, first mate of the *Pequod,* views the "Anacharsis Clootz deputation" as a "heathen crew that have small touch of human mothers in them." They are "whelped by the sharkish seas" (VII, 211). No doubt his attitude is directed primarily toward the dark-skinned harpooneers—the Polynesian Queequeg, the Negro Daggoo, the American Indian Tashtego —and the Oriental Fedallah. Brown, black, red, and yellow, these "pagan leopards," as Captain Ahab calls them, are stock gothic types. James E. Miller calls them "sons of darkness."[7] Leslie Fiedler sees them as "rather emblems than characters."[8]

And, to some extent, Ronald Mason's estimate of Fedallah applies to other pagans: "It is difficult to escape the suspicion that Melville took him ready-made from stock . . . ; trading perhaps involuntarily upon the fashionable vogue . . . of imparting the mysterious East for good measure of *diablerie* into familiar Western settings frequently for no better purpose than to make the flesh creep."[9] Considered together, all the harpooneers are intended to make Western "flesh creep." They remain unappalled and unimpressed by such omens as the "plaintively wild and unearthly" cry in the night. As the *Pequod's* stokers before the try-works, they are satanic figures: ". . . The harpooneers wildly gesticulated with their huge pronged forks and dippers; as the wind howled on, and the sea leaped, and the ship groaned and dived, and yet steadfastly shot her red hell further and further into the blackness of the sea and the night" (VIII, 180). In their unholy blood Captain Ahab baptizes his harpoon. The emphasis on their darkness, their heathenishness and barbarity makes them stock figures of evil. Like Samoa and Bembo, they are "none of your effeminate barbarians."

But "Hark ye yet again,—the little lower layer." All three (Fedallah is an exception and will be dealt with later), though darkly diabolic, are also magnificent physical specimens of humanity; all three, though, or because, they are savage, possess an earthiness, a simple integrity, a poise and dedication— traits all too lacking in their immediate superiors, the white mates. Each, as Vincent notes, "is a human soul, to be respected in its individuality."[10] The respect elicited by the pagan harpooneers makes them proper children of Ishmael's "just Spirit of Equality."

The most glowing example of "that democratic dignity which "radiates without end from God" is Starbuck's harpooneer and Ishmael's close friend Queequeg. Typical of the response this savage Prince of Rokovoko evokes from readers is that of William Sedgwick, who calls Queequeg "perhaps the one loveable character in the whole book."[11] In part, his attractiveness echoes Tommo's loving description of the Marquesans, and, like them, Queequeg, as well as the other pagans, bears traces of the noble savage convention; but romantic convention is far outweighed by their roles as believable seamen sharing with the others common duties. As noted in connection with *Typee,* literary convention in Melville's treatment of the savage is dismissed by most critics who prefer, instead, to regard Melville's attitude as a reasoned one based on experience. Vincent will suffice here: "Neither Queequeg nor *Typee* is a sentimental, Pierre Loti flight from reality. . . . Melville was too realistic to perpetuate in fiction the myth of the goodness of natural man."[12]

Physically, at least, Queequeg is no "natural man." Like Samoa, he is a horror. His "unearthly" complexion—"purplish-yellow"—is made more repelling by the "large, blacklish-looking squares" of tattooing. His bald purplish head, with only "a small scalp-knot twisted up on his forehead" looks "like a mildewed skull." Intensifying the "devil" image, Queequeg carries the appropriate props—an embalmed head and a wicked-looking tomahawk. No wonder Ishmael shudders at his first glimpse of Queequeg; for, like Samoa, the native "is a very devil to behold."

Thus far Melville seems prepared to play variations on the man-devil duality; Queequeg's human traits, however, soon relegate the satanic features to the level of trappings. Ishmael is quick to note the irrelevance of a man's exterior: "It's only his outside; a man can be honest in any sort of skin" (vii, 26). A more studied observation follows Ishmael's spending the night with the Polynesian: "Savage though he was, and hideously marred about the face . . . his countenance yet had something in it which was by no means disagreeable. You cannot hide the soul" (vii, 60). As the narrator of *Mardi* phrased it, "Though beauty be obvious, the only loveliness is invisible" (p. 99). Discovering the ironic contradiction between appearance and fact, Ishmael continues with a warm tribute to the Polynesian:

Through all his unearthly tattooings, I thought I saw the traces of a simple honest heart; and in his large, deep eyes, fiery black and

bold, there seemed tokens of a spirit that would dare a thousand
devils. And besides all this, there was a certain lofty bearing about
the pagan, which even his uncouthness could not altogether maim.
He looked like a man who had never cringed and never had had
a creditor. Whether it was, too, that his head being shaved, his
forehead was drawn out in freer and brighter relief, and looked
more expansive than it otherwise would, this I will not venture to
decide; but certain it was his head was phrenologically an excellent
one. It may seem ridiculous, but it reminded me of General Washington's head, as seen in the popular busts of him. It had the same
long regularly graded retreating slope from above the brows, which
were likewise very projecting, like two long promontories thickly
wooded on top. Queequeg was George Washington cannibalisti-
cally developed. [VII, 60–61]

Queequeg's "lofty bearing," his "never cringing," his "expansive forehead," his resemblance to Washington—all emphasize the pride, dignity, and strength of a man. Virtually every
time that Ishmael talks of Queequeg, his remarks are characterized by admiration and respect. Queequeg has "royal stuff"
in his veins; he is a "sea Prince of Wales," a "grand and glori-
ous fellow" possessed of "miraculous dexterity and strength."
He is "essentially polite" and has "an innate sense of delicacy."
Thus, Queequeg's devilish appearance becomes subordinate
to his human attributes; one recognizes, along with Ishmael,
that "the man's a human being just as I am" (VII, 30).

Ishmael's evaluation is not mere gratuitous praise; Queequeg's actions testify to the validity of Ishmael's words. We
learn of his "desperate dauntlessness" in desiring to see the
Christian world[13] and of his "profound" determination to
learn Christian ways so that he might enlighten his countrymen and learn the arts "whereby to make his people still
happier than they were; and more than that, still better than
they were." Instead, he learns, as did Tommo, that Christians
could be miserable and wicked, "infinitely more so, than all
his father's heathens" (VII, 69), and that contact with them
made him unfit for ascending his island throne. His discovery
answers the question raised by White-Jacket: "Are there no
Moravians in the Moon, that not a missionary has yet visited
this poor pagan planet of ours, to civilize civilization and

christianize Christendom?" (p. 267). We see him, too, display great presence of mind and courage aboard the packet from New Bedford to Nantucket when the vessel's boom breaks loose and, wildly sweeping the after deck, jeopardizes everyone aboard. When one person is knocked into the sea, ". . . all hands were in a panic; and to attempt snatching at the boom to stay it, seemed madness. . . . Nothing was done, and nothing seemed capable of being done" (vii, 75). Queequeg, however, deftly and calmly lassoes the boom and secures it to the bulwarks. Not yet done, he plunges into the sea and rescues the "greenhorn" knocked overboard—an act which anticipates his more daring rescue of Tashtego, who, encased in a whale's head drifting to the bottom of the Indian Ocean, appears hopelessly lost until Queequeg's "courage and great skill" effect a "noble rescue."

Ishmael's reaction to Queequeg's saving the "greenhorn" is sufficient testimony to the stature of the pagan, and it points toward a recognition, not just of Queequeg's humanness, but of the interdependence of all men:

Was there ever such unconsciousness? He did not seem to think that he at all deserved a medal from the Humane and Magnanimous Societies. He only asked for water—fresh water—something to wipe the brine off; that done, he put on dry clothes, lighted his pipe, and leaning against the bulwarks, and mildly eyeing those around him, seemed to be saying to himself—"It's a mutual, joint-stock world, in all meridians. We cannibals must help these Christians." [vii, 76]

In Queequeg's spirit, in his heroism that admits of no self-glorification, Ishmael sees the shining possibilities of man and recognizes the practicality and beauty of such a man enjoying a "divine equality."

Whereas Queequeg possesses Samoa's hideous appearance and dauntless spirit, he is not a humorous figure. Two incidents involving Queequeg could, in themselves, smack of comic patronizing, but Melville turns them toward an ironic criticism of white Christian civilization. In his manner of dressing himself, Queequeg could easily be the object of

laughter. With a tall beaver hat on his head but still minus
his trousers, he crawls under the bed and, with "sundry violent graspings and strainings," pulls on—his boots! Queequeg
is touched just enough by Christian morality to emulate Western modesty—civilized just enough to regard his naked heels
and toes as obscenities. Indirectly, Melville echoes the criticism in *Typee* and *Omoo* of the white man's crusade to im-
pose his moral standards on the primitives. Rather than smile
at Queequeg, one is more inclined to regret what amounts to
a tarnishing, by white influence, of his natural innocence and
aplomb. On another occasion, Queequeg tells Ishmael a
"funny story" of how, when not wishing to seem ignorant of
the precise use of the wheelbarrow, he shouldered the barrow
and walked up the wharf. Ishmael's response—"Why, Queequeg, you might have known better than that, one would
think. Didn't the people laugh?"—affords Queequeg the
chance to offer an object lesson in mutual understanding:

The people of his island of Rokovoko, it seems, at their wedding
feasts express the fragrant water of young cocoa-nuts into a large
stained calabash like a punch-bowl; and this punch-bowl always
forms the great central ornament on the braided mat where the
feast is held. Now a certain grand merchant ship once touched at
Rokovoko, and its commander—from all accounts a very stately
punctilious gentleman, at least for a sea-captain—this commander
was invited to the wedding feast of Queequeg's sister. . . . Well;
when all the wedding guests were assembled at the bride's bamboo
cottage, this captain marches in, and being assigned the post of
honour, placed himself over against the punch-bowl, and between
the High Priest and his majesty the King, Queequeg's father. Grace
being said . . . the High Priest opens the banquet by the immemo-
rial ceremony of the island; that is, dipping his consecrated and
consecrating fingers into the bowl before the blessed beverage cir-
culates. Seeing himself placed next the Priest, and noting the ceremony, and thinking himself—being captain of a ship—as having
plain precedence over a mere island King, especially in the King's
own house—the captain cooly proceeds to wash his hands in the
punch-bowl;—taking it, I suppose, for a huge finger-glass. "Now,"
said Queequeg, "what you tink now?—Didn't our people laugh?"
[VII, 72–73]

Ishmael offers no comment, but the lesson is clear: the barbarian among whites is no more inferior or ridiculous than is

the white man among barbarians. Again, a point of contact with *Mardi* is evident; the whole episode recalls the natives both in that book and in *Omoo* laughing at the ridiculous appearance of the whites. If anything, the "finger bowl" episode reinforces Taji's call for mutual respect: "Away with our stares and grimaces. The New Zealander's tattooing is not a prodigy; nor the Chinaman's way an enigma. No custom is strange; no creed is absurd" (pp. 12–13). Neither Ishmael nor his readers can smile comfortably at and feel superior to the heathen. Such condescension would but confirm Miller's observation that "in Ishmael's world Christians act like savages and savages like Christians"[14]—an ironic contradiction between appearance and fact already recognized by Melville's earlier heroes. Certainly, Queequeg's unselfish rescue of both the greenhorn and Tashtego is Christian, in the practical sense of the word. In addition, his simple, honest heart, natural sagacity, and poise, traits which Tommo found lacking in Western civilization, combine to form "a nature in which there lurked no civilized hypocrisies and bland deceits" (VII, 62). He is earthy, natural man, the embodiment of the wisdom of Solomon, the reputed author of Ecclesiastes: "There is nothing better for a man, than that he should eat and drink, and that he should make his soul enjoy good in his labor."[15] Thus, the human, not the heathen, is further emphasized in Queequeg. One can readily understand Ishmael's decision "to try a pagan friend . . . since Christian kindness has proved but hollow courtesy" (VII, 62).

Even before Ishmael sails, he has ample evidence of the refreshing alternative to the "wolfish world" which Queequeg presents. Most notable, perhaps, is the oblique criticism of Christian worship made by Queequeg's religion. The Whaleman's Chapel of New Bedford, visited by Ishmael and Queequeg, the latter with "a wondering gaze of incredulous curiosity in his countenance," is an apt counterpart to Ishmael's "damp, drizzly November" soul. "Frigid inscriptions" on black-bordered cenotaphs, a painting depicting "a gallant ship beating against a terrible storm off a lee coast of black

rocks and snowy breakers," a congregation "scattered" in
isolated pockets about the chapel, a minister whose physical
isolation in the pulpit signifies "his spiritual withdrawal . . .
from all outward worldly ties and connections," a hymn
threatening the "opening maw of hell," a sermon emphasizing the black terrors awaiting the disobedient—together
these elements create an image of religion harsh in its bleak-
ness and stark obedience to a vengeful god but void of
human love and brotherhood. Queequeg leaves the service
(either he is bored or his incredulity is stretched too far),
and Ishmael offers no comment on it; but, indirectly, a comment is forthcoming in the chapter immediately following,
wherein we see Queequeg's form of worship. The juxtaposition invites comparison. Queequeg's service is a simple ceremony in which he pays simple homage to a little Negro idol,
Yojo. Generosity (signified by the offering presented to
Yojo) and love (suggested by Queequeg's salaaming before
and kissing the idol) replace the fear dominant in the Whaleman's Chapel. It is a service which calls for mutual respect,
a service which brings together the brown savage and the
white outcast, a service which touchingly exemplifies the
practical implementation of Christianity. Ishmael, a spectator
in the grim Christian chapel, offers his observations as par-
ticipant in Queequeg's church. They are worth repeating in
full:

I was a good Christian; born and bred in the bosom of the infallible Presbyterian Church. How then could I unite with this
wild idolater in worshipping his piece of wood? But what is worship? thought I. Do you suppose now, Ishmael, that the magnanimous God of heavens and earth—pagans and all included—can
possibly be jealous of an insignificant bit of black wood? Impossible! But what is worship?—to do the will of God?—*that* is worship. And what is the will of God?—to do to my fellow-man what
I would have my fellow-man to do to *me*—*that* is the will of God.
Now, Queequeg is my fellow-man. And what do I wish that this
Queequeg would do to me? Why, unite with me in my particular
Presbyterian form of worship. Consequently, I must then unite
with him in his; ergo, I must turn idolater. So I kindled the shav-
ings; helped prop up the innocent little idol; offered him burnt
biscuit with Queequeg; salaamed before him twice or thrice; kissed

his nose; and that done we undressed and went to bed, at peace with our own consciences and all the world. [VII, 64]

This dramatization of the Golden Rule,[16] a dramatization touched by warmth, tolerance, and love between a tattooed savage and a despairing white man, associates the pagan religion with the beauty of Christian brotherhood. Ironically, the Christian's religion, which professes a love for one's fellow men, admits of no human interdependence. As Vincent neatly puts it, "The sunlight of Polynesia drove the November drizzle of New England Calvinism from his [Ishmael's] soul."[17]

The difference between the pagan and the civilized worlds is also reflected in Ishmael's reaction to Queequeg's display of friendship. Again, the incident occurs after Ishmael's exposure to the Whaleman's Chapel. Together they share Queequeg's pipe, after which the native professes unbridled affection for Ishmael; they become "bosom friends." Ishmael comments, "In a countryman this sudden flame of friendship would have seemed far too premature, a thing to be much distrusted; but in this simple savage those old rules would not apply" (VII, 63). Queequeg's spontaneous "flame of friendship" glows in warm contrast to the cold isolation of the civilized world.

Queequeg's rescue of the "greenhorn" off the Nantucket packet should be amplified here, for it is preceded by an incident which is a revealing comment on race relations. The man Queequeg rescues is one of those who earlier jeered at the spectacle of "two fellow beings"—Queequeg and Ishmael—being "so companionable." And there were others:

... some boobies and bumpkins ... who, by their intense greenness, must have come from the heart and centre of all verdure. Queequeg caught one of these young saplings mimicking him behind his back. I thought the bumpkin's hour of doom was come. Dropping his harpoon, the brawny savage caught him in his arms, and by an almost miraculous dexterity and strength, sent him high up bodily into the air; then slightly tapping his stern in midsomerset, the fellow landed with bursting lungs upon his feet, while Queequeg, turning his back upon him, lighted his tomahawk-pipe and passed it to me for a puff. [VII, 74]

The incident provokes several observations. First, it is an interesting echo of a similar situation in *Redburn,* i.e., Lavender and a white woman walking arm-in-arm down a Liverpool street. That the jeerers here are "from the heart and centre of all verdure" emphasizes the validity of Redburn's admission that his surprise at seeing a black man with a white woman could be attributed to his "local" prejudices. We recall, too, that Redburn sees in the arm-in-arm relationship the black man's claim "to humanity and normal equality"—the same claim which the bond between Ishmael and Queequeg confirms. And in the contrast between the English indifference to the mixed couple and the American stares and grimaces, we find painful confirmation of Redburn's recognition of how Americans neglect "the principle that stands at the head of our Declaration of Independence." Second, Queequeg's quickness to violence parallels the retaliatory actions of the nonwhites discussed earlier in this study. As in those cases, the nonwhite responds to the white man's insult with what appears to be instinctive hostility. Miller calls Queequeg's rashness here "his ultimate weakness" which "renders him finally deficient—like the virtuous but fickle savages of *Typee* and *Omoo.*"[18] The insult which causes Queequeg's hostility to flash, however, is a denial of his claim to humanity. Queequeg is motivated not by instinctive hostility but by man's instinctive sense of his own dignity. He can hardly be condemned as subhuman when what he is essentially asserting is the inviolability of the human personality. If anyone is to be condemned, it is the white man who, as Tommo notes, "exasperated the Polynesians into savages." Queequeg's "savagery," however, is considerably undercut by the obvious playfulness of his threat and by his subsequent contempt for the fellow: " 'Kill-e,' cried Queequeg, twisting his tattooed face into an unearthly expression of disdain, 'ah! him bevy small-e fish-e; Queequeg no-kill-e so small-e fish-e; Queequeg kill-e big whale!' " (vii, 74–75). Add to this his utter selflessness in rescuing this bumpkin, and Queequeg emerges from the episode with his stature as a

man and his earthy brand of Christianity intact. The greenhorn may call Queequeg "the devil," but the Polynesian
clearly stands a man. The whole episode dramatically confirms Ishmael's response to the incredulous stares and grimaces at the companionship of a white man and a native:
". . . as though a white man were anything more dignified
than a whitewashed negro" (VII, 74).

During the chapter entitled "The First Lowering" Starbuck's boat, of which Queequeg and Ishmael are a part, is
swamped and subsequently isolated from the other boats and
the *Pequod* in the awesome blackness of the night sea, made
more terrifying by the driving scud and rack. The scene is
the painting in the Whaleman's Chapel come to life: "The
wind increased to a howl; the waves dashed their bucklers
together; the whole squall roared, forked, and crackled
around us like a white fire upon the prairie, in which, un-
consumed, we were burning; immortal in these jaws of
death!" (VII, 284). In the midst "of that almighty forlornness," Queequeg raises a lantern attached to a waif-pole. Ishmael's account of this pathetic but somehow beautiful act
strikes to the very heart of his relationship with Queequeg:
"There, then, he sat, the sign and symbol of a man without
faith, hopelessly holding up hope in the midst of despair" (VII,
284). It is this brown savage who, though faithless, brings
to Ishmael the saving light of "hope"—hope in the affirma-
tive possibilities of human interdependence. The bond between the white outcast and the brown heathen is a precious
testimony to the beauty of interracial brotherhood.

As has been noted, Ishmael's mood when he goes to sea
is one of controlled desperation. Specifically, we know little
of his condition on land; it is tempting, however, to speculate.
"Nothing particular" interests him on shore, where he has
grown "grim about the mouth" (probably controlling his
antagonism toward others, e.g., knocking off their hats). As
mentioned, he is acutely aware of the isolated existence. His
name recalls Abraham's banished son, whose "hand will be
against every man, and every man's hand against him." Con-

sidering these implications, it is not difficult to account for
Ishmael's November soul; he is alone. That Queequeg is the
man through whom Ishmael is restored to the world and with
whom Ishmael rediscovers the meaning of Christian brotherhood is an object lesson in interracial dependency rivaled in
nineteenth-century American fiction only by the relationship
between Huck Finn and Nigger Jim.

Queequeg is not long in initiating Ishmael's rebirth. After
the first night in New Bedford, during which they are compelled to share a bed, Ishmael awakens to find Queequeg's
arm thrown over him "in the most loving and affectionate
manner." The knot is beginning to be tied, at least by the
savage. As Ishmael observes, "You had almost thought I had
been his wife" (VII, 31). Ishmael has initial misgivings, but
they vanish when he returns from the bleak chapel through
the mist-shrouded, sleet-driven New Bedford streets. In the
room, warmed by a fire, Ishmael watches his roommate; he,
too, is warmed by "strange feelings": "I felt a melting in me.
No more my splintered heart and maddened hand were
turned against the wolfish world. This soothing savage had
redeemed it" (VII, 62). The two begin to merge into one,
sharing life stories, thoughts, Queequeg's pipe, and a common bed; and Ishmael admits "how elastic our stiff prejudices
grow when love once comes to bend them" (VII, 66). How
ironic that the savage, conventionally stereotyped as an animal, should embody love—a quality evidently lacking in
Ishmael's "wolfish" (and Christian) world.[19] And just as
Queequeg redeems Ishmael's heart, his coffin literally redeems
Ishmael when the *Pequod* and its entire crew are destroyed.
Alone again, this time in the vast Pacific, Ishmael is buoyed
up by his friend's coffin, carved to resemble Queequeg. The
man who in life held the lantern of hope reaches from beyond
death to grant Ishmael his life.

The bond formed in New Bedford is metaphysically tight-
ened at sea. As Queequeg's bowsman, Ishmael is responsible
for vigilantly safeguarding his pagan friend during the process
of "cutting in." While Queequeg precariously scrambles over

the back of a whale tied ten feet below the deck and sur-
rounded by ravenous sharks and Ishmael stands at the bulwarks of the *Pequod,* a monkey-rope tied to both men unites
them into "an elongated Siamese ligature." In the union,
Ishmael observes, "Queequeg was my own inseparable twin
brother" (VIII, 48). The metaphor of the monkey-rope uniting
a brown man with a white becomes a moving and recurring
symbol of the interdependence of all men. In the oft-quoted
words of Ishmael, that interdependence is readily apparent:

So strongly and metaphysically did I conceive of my situation then,
that while earnestly watching his motions, I seemed distinctly to
perceive that my own individuality was now merged in a joint
stock company of two: that my free will had received a mortal
wound; and that another's mistake or misfortune might plunge
innocent me into unmerited disaster and death. Therefore, I saw
that here was a sort of interregnum in Providence; for its even-
handed equity never could have sanctioned so gross an injustice.
And yet still further pondering—while I jerked him now and then
from between the whale and the ship, which would threaten to jam
him—still further pondering, I say, I saw that this situation of
mine was the precise situation of every mortal that breathes; only,
in most cases, he, one way or other, has this Siamese connection
with a plurality of other mortals. [VIII, 48–49]

Watching Queequeg below him, half-hidden in the shark-
infested and bloodied waters, Ishmael raises a question which
echoes his earlier belief in the "just Spirit of Equality": "Well,
well, my dear comrade and twin brother. . . . Are you not the
precious image of each and all of us men in this whaling
world?" (VIII, 50). On the basis of Queequeg's character, his
actions, his redemption of Ishmael, one is compelled to answer
for the Polynesian—yes. White Ishmael and brown Queequeg,
twin brothers and images of the creator, they form a beautiful example of interracial understanding, respect, and love.
Through their union Melville has dramatized how the races
should and could relate.

Harpooneer to the third mate Flask is a black member of
the Clootz deputation—the "negro-savage" Daggoo. Like the
other primitives, he helps contribute to the Gothic mood of
the book. During a violent thunderstorm he stands "relieved

against the ghostly light" and, looming up "to thrice his real stature," seems "the black cloud from which the thunder had come" (VIII, 280). Also, Melville surrounds him with suggestions of bestiality: he is "erect as a giraffe"; his bulk shakes the cabin "as when an African elephant goes passenger in a ship"; his tread is "lion-like"; he snuffs the air through "dilated nostrils." His actions, too, suggest savagery. On a whim he thrusts the steward's head into a trencher, and he engages in a brawl with a Spanish sailor. Thus far, then, Daggoo seems "devilish dark."

As noted before, however, Melville adds another dimension to his nonwhite characters, tending to make human those who would otherwise be stereotypes. Daggoo is no exception. He is "wonderfully abstemious," a somewhat incongruous trait in a "savage." He acts quickly to save his fellow harpooneer Tashtego from death and is overjoyed when Queequeg effects the rescue. He is most memorable, however, in his physical magnitude. He is a black colossus—a "gigantic," "broad," and "superb person." Offsetting the animal images are the many suggestions of royalty attached to him. Ishmael notes his "barbaric majesty" and "lordly chest" and calls him "baronial," "a noble negro," and an "imperial negro." On several occasions Ishmael refers to Daggoo as Ahasuerus— the biblical king who "reigned from India even unto Ethiopia" and who decreed "that every man should bear rule in his own house." The whites stand starkly insignificant beside him. Third mate Flask, astride the shoulders of Daggoo, seems "a snow flake on his broad back," and "the bearer looked nobler than the rider" (VII, 279). Again, Flask looks "like a chessman beside him." Not just Flask, but any "white man before him seemed a white flag come to beg truce of a fortress" (VII, 149). Although physical superiority is not necessarily a measure of a man, Ishmael offers an observation which associates physical brawn not only with beauty but also with respect:

Real strength never impairs beauty or harmony, but it often bestows it; and in everything imposingly beautiful, strength has much to do with the magic. Take away the tied tendons that all over seem bursting from the marble in the carved Hercules, and its charm would be gone. As devout Eckermann lifted the linen sheet from the naked corpse of Goethe, he was overwhelmed with the massive chest of the man, that seemed as a Roman triumphal arch. When Angelo paints even God the Father in human form, mark what robustness is there. And whatever they may reveal of the divine love in the Son, the soft, curled, hermaphroditical Italian pictures, in which his idea has been most successfully embodied; these pictures, so destitute as they are of all brawniness, hint nothing of any power, but the mere negative, feminine one of submission and endurance, which on all hands it is conceded, form the peculiar practical virtues of his teachings. [VIII, 119]

"Submission and endurance," appropriate attitudes for the traditional Negro, are alien to Daggoo. Pride and defiance mark his actions, particularly in a scene reminiscent of Bembo's fight with Sidney Ben. The night watch, still stirred by drink and their captain's fierce exhortations to pursue his vengeance, find their carousing threatened by an approaching squall. An old Manx sailor sees an ominous parallel between Captain Ahab and the "pitch black" sky. Daggoo's reply reflects his contempt for the white man's superstition and underscores his pride in the strength his color connotes:[20] "What of that? Who's afraid of black's afraid of me! I'm quarried out of it!" (VII, 219). A Spanish sailor, however, sees black not as a symbol of strength but as the traditional color of evil: "Ay, harpooneer, thy race is the undeniable dark side of mankind—devilish dark at that." He is quick to add, "No offense," to which Daggoo grimly replies, "None." But the Spaniard will not let "the old grudge" die; he must resort to the racial insult. To a sailor's question, "What's that I saw —lightning?" the Spaniard replies, "No; Daggoo showing his teeth." Daggoo's answer to the stock Negro insult is to spring on the Spaniard, shouting, "Swallow thine, manikin! White skin, white liver!" (VII, 220). Thus, a pattern evident as early in *Typee* repeats itself: the white man insults; the dark, defending against the assault on his human dignity, retaliates. Worth mentioning here is that the Spaniard quickly resorts to a dagger, an act met with a sailor's shout for "fair play." The

sailors form a ring around the combatants, while the chorus-
like Manxman observes, "In that ring Cain struck Abel.
Sweet work, right work! No? Why then, God, mad'st thou
the ring?" (vii, 221). The question is skeptical enough—
why does God permit the clash between brothers? If an answer is to be found, it lies in the union between Ishmael and
Queequeg, who, in their mutual respect, illustrate a compati-
ble relationship between men of different colors. At any rate,
the scene is an illustration of the ugliness of racial prejudice;
it is most memorable for Daggoo's response—a response constituting his refutation of the traditional evil of blackness and
his assertion of his human dignity.

What seems most significant about Daggoo is that, though
a Negro, he possesses none of the previously established
"darky" characteristics. Superior to the whites in physique,
daring and proud of spirit, he commands both awe and
respect. He is a man; he could also be Melville's example of
what the Negro, free from the white man's lash, could be.
Appropriately enough, Daggoo is relatively untouched by
white civilization, "having never been anywhere in the world
but in Africa, Nantucket, and the pagan harbours most frequented by whalemen" (vii, 148). In effect, the white man
has not reduced him to a brute or to a cringing subservient.
His manhood, his image of God, remains intact; accordingly,
he, like Queequeg, is a child of the "just Spirit of Equality."

Harpooneer to the second mate Stubb is the red member
of the Clootz deputation, the "wild" Gay Head Indian Tashtego. Like the other pagans, he is cast in the mold of the
devilish savage. With "snaky limbs" and gleaming "shark
white teeth," Tashtego, "nimble as a cat," seems the descend-
ant of the Puritans' Black Man—"the Prince of the Powers
of the Air." Darting his fork at the steward and threatening
to scalp him, Tashtego shows a grim, humorous contempt for
the cowardly white.

Physically, Tashtego evokes admiration. With "long, lean,
sable hair, high cheek bones," and eyes "like fixed stars"—
"antarctic in their glittering expression"—he is an appropri-

ate "inheritor of the unvitiated blood of those proud warrior hunters, who, in quest for the great New England moose, had scoured, bow in hand, the aboriginal forests of the main" (VII, 148). This inheritance is emphasized by Tashtego's prominence atop the mainmast as lookout for Leviathan, a picture which draws from Ishmael this impressive description:

High aloft in the cross-trees was that mad Gay-Header, Tashtego. His body was reaching eagerly forward, his hand stretched out like a wand, and at brief sudden intervals he continued his cries. To be sure, the same sound was that very moment perhaps being heard all over the seas, from hundreds of whalemen's look-outs perched as high in the air; but from few of those lungs could that accustomed old cry have derived such a marvellous cadence as from Tashtego the Indian's. [VII, 270]

As his position in the mainmast suggests, Tashtego carries himself above his white fellows. Like the other harpooneers, he is unmoved by the omens which visit the cruising *Pequod*. During the revel which precedes the Spaniard-Daggoo fight, he remains quietly aloof, offering only a contemptuous observation of the jigging sailors: "That's a white man; he calls that fun: humph! I save my sweat" (VII, 217). As for the fight itself and the approaching squall, he stoically asserts his indifference: "A row alow, and a row aloft—Gods and men—both brawlers! Humph!" (VII, 220).

Tashtego is an Isolato from the "last remnant of a village of red men." Whether he realizes his debt to Queequeg is not known, but Queequeg's saving him from a watery death is a part of the federation aboard the *Pequod*. Easily overlooked in the federation is Tashtego's skillful and active participation in the business of whaling, an enterprise requiring the coordinated efforts of all the crew. Sharing "common duties, common dangers and common feelings," Tashtego and the rest of the federation, as R. E. Watters notes, "subordinate . . . their egos to assist their fellow man, Ahab."[21] Hence, Tashtego remains in the mind as a faint echo of the dual-natured savages found frequently in Melville's works—instinctive and animalistic, but also able and proud. Whether we regard him as an integral member of the crew, all of whose individualities are welded into oneness, or as man alone who is "a wonder, a grandeur, and a woe," he, too, hovering high above the *Pequod* and "eagerly peering toward the horizon," is a child of the "just Spirit of Equality."

From the brown, black, and red harpooneers, we move to a yellow man, Ahab's harpooneer Fedallah. "Man," however, is an inappropriate term for him; it is even difficult to call him a character, for he lacks the human traits which raise the other pagans above the level of gothic types. A sampling of criticism suggests general agreement that Fedallah is not a flesh-and-blood member of the *Pequod's* crew. To F. O. Matthiessen, he is "the typically exaggerated product of romantic Satanism."[22] Ronald Mason sees him as "the nearest to pinchback melodrama that Melville comes in this great story."[23] Leslie Fiedler states, "Parsee is not really a character at all . . ." but "a conventional device for portraying inwardness, a projected nightmare."[24] Newton Arvin calls him "a principle of pure negation, of hatred instead of love, vindictiveness instead of charity, destruction instead of creativeness."[25] Henry A. Murray simply dismisses him as "superfluous," and as a representation of "the cool, heartless, cunning, calculating, intellectual Devil of the medieval mythmakers."[26] Certainly, the details surrounding Fedallah remove him from the human family. He and his phantom followers are "of that vivid, tiger-yellow complexion peculiar to some of the aboriginal natives of the Manillas;—a race notorious for a certain diabolism of subtlety" (VII, 273). Sea tradition places them as "agents on the water of the devil, their lord." Fedallah's single white tooth "evilly protruding from steellike lips" is seen by Flask as "a snake's head." Fedallah's reply to Ahab at one time is "half-hissed." Stubb calls him "the devil in disguise." The men in general are uncertain of whether he is "mortal substance" or "a tremulous shadow cast upon the deck by some unseen being's body." In essence, he is the shadow of Ahab's soul, linked to him as the weird sisters are to Macbeth. Shadow, device, convention, principle, agent—call him what one will, Fedallah is not a "man." Unlike the other harpooneers who, by virtue of their manly appearance, their genuinely human traits, or both, emerge as men, Fedallah is a "devil." It is possible that the union between Ahab and the Parsee exemplifies a sinister interdependence which defines another dimension of the federation aboard the *Pequod;* but Ahab clearly does not need him, as Fedallah's death has no effect on Ahab's purpose. Further, since the Parsee is a shadowy abstraction while Ahab "has his humanities," it would be dangerous to view their relationship in racial or human terms.

From the awesome pagan squires who thrill to the plunge of the whaleboat and to the deadly thrust of the harpoon, we turn now to the chief domestic of the *Pequod*—the master of the galley, the old, black Fleece. Indolent and dim-witted, Fleece takes his place alongside Melville's early sea cooks, Baltimore, Mr. Thompson, and Old Coffee, as an object of humor derived from crude popular tradition. He appears only once, in a scene with Stubb, a scene Matthiessen calls "comic relief";[27] from his very entrance the darky joke, complete with wretched pun, is obvious:

The old black, not in any very high glee at having been previously roused from his warm hammock at a most unseasonable hour, came shambling along from his galley, for, like many old blacks, there was something the matter with his knee-pans, which he did not keep well scoured like his other pans; this old Fleece, as they called him, came shuffling and limping along, assisting his step with his tongs, which, after a clumsy fashion, were made of straightened iron hoops; this old Ebony floundered along, and in obedience to the word of command, came to a dead stop on the opposite side of Stubb's sideboard; when, with both hands folded before him, and resting on his two-legged cane, he bowed his arched back still further over, at the same time sideways inclining his head, so as to bring his best ear into play. [VIII, 14–15]

The stage is set, with the crotchety old darky listening for the master's voice. Repeating the word "cook" in what Richard Chase calls "that form of direct address which characterized the humor of the time,"[28] master Stubb begins, first berating Fleece for the poorly cooked whale steak, then ordering him to preach a sermon to quiet the sharks noisily feeding on the

dead whale tied to the ship. Sullenly, Fleece goes to the bulwarks and, looking down, addresses "his congregation" in a
dialect obviously intended for humor:

"Fellow-critters: I'se ordered here to say dat you must stop dat
dam noise dare. You hear? Stop dat dam smackin' ob de lip!
Massa Stubb say dat you can fill your dam bellies up to de hatch-
ings, but by Gor! you must stop dat dam racket!" [VIII, 15]

As the scene progresses, Stubb is the straight-man interlocutor and Fleece the slow-witted, sullenly obedient end man:

"Cook," here interposed Stubb, accompanying the word with a
sudden slap on the shoulder,—"Cook! why, damn your eyes, you
mustn't swear that way when you're preaching. That's no way to
convert sinners, cook!" [VIII, 16]

And Fleece continues:

Do you is all sharks, and by natur wery woracious, yet I say to
you, fellow-critters, dat dat woraciousness—'top dat dam slappin'
ob de tail! How you tink to hear, s'pose you keep up such a dam
slappin' and bitin' dare? [VIII, 16]

The sermon and the bad joke continue until Stubb orders the
benediction; Fleece dutifully complies:

Cussed fellow-critters! Kick up de damndest row as ever you can;
fill your dam' bellies till day bust—and den die. [VIII, 17]

Still, Stubb has not had his fill, and the minstrel show goes
on with Fleece the butt of jokes as rank as the dead whale
(and probably as old). Stubb unmercifully prods the sulky
black:

"Now, cook," said Stubb, resuming his supper at the capstan;
"stand just where you stood before, there, over against me, and
pay particular attention."
"All 'dention," said Fleece, again stooping over upon his tongs
in the desired position.
"Well," said Stubb, helping himself freely meanwhile; "I shall
now go back to the subject of this steak. In the first place, how
old are you, cook?"
"What dat do wid de 'teak" said the old black testily.
"Silence! How old are you, cook?"
" 'Bout ninety, dey say," he gloomily muttered.
"And have you lived in this world hard upon one hundred
years, cook, and don't know yet how to cook a whale-steak?"

rapidly belting another mouthful at the last word, so that that morsel seemed a continuation of the question. "Where were you born, cook?"

" 'Hind de hatchway, in ferry-boat, goin' ober de Roanoke." [VIII, 17]

More jokes, at the expense of the darky's stupidity, follow; the tasteless scene speaks for itself:

"Cook," said Stubb, squaring himself once more; "do you belong to the church?"

"Passed one once in Cape-Town," said the old man sullenly.

"And you have once in your life passed a holy church in Cape-Town, where you doubtless overheard a holy parson addressing his hearers as his beloved fellow creatures, have you, cook? And yet you come here, and tell me such a dreadful lie as you did just now, eh?" said Stubb. "Where do you expect to go to, cook?"

"Go to bed berry soon," he mumbled, half turning as he spoke.

"Avast! heave to! I mean when you die, cook. It's an awful question. Now what's your answer?"

"When dis old brack man dies," said the negro slowly, changing his whole air and demeanour, "he hisself won't go nowhere; but some bressed angel will come and fetch him."

"Fetch him? How? In a coach and four, as they fetched Elijah? And fetch him where?"

"Up dere," said Fleece, holding his tongs straight over his head, and keeping it there very solemnly.

"So, then, you expect to go up into our maintop, do you, cook, when you are dead? But don't you know the higher you climb the colder it gets? Maintop, eh?"

"Didn't say dat't all," said Fleece, again in the sulks.

"You said up there, didn't you? and now look yourself, and see where your tongs are pointing. But, perhaps you expect to get into heaven by crawling through the lubber's hold, cook; but, no, no, cook, you don't get there, except you go the regular way, round by the rigging. It's a ticklish business, but must be done, or else it's no go. But none of us are in heaven yet. Drop your tongs, cook, and hear my orders. Do ye hear? Hold your hat in one hand, and clap t'other atop of your heart, when I'm giving my orders, cook. What! that your heart, there?—that's your gizzard! Aloft! aloft!—that's it—now you have it. Hold it there now, and pay attention." [VIII, 18–191]

The impression of Fleece follows the general pattern of the previous sea cooks—indolent, stupid, subservient—but differences do exist. His sulking and occasional balking at Stubb's commands set him apart from the completely docile

Baltimore; his swearing distinguishes him from the pious Mr. Thompson; and he lacks the mock dignity of his predecessors and the jolly good spirits of Old Coffee's assistants. He appears, too, to have a much more serious function than do the others. If he is a "figure of fun" as Warner Berthoff notes,[29] the fun is outweighed by Stubb's insensitive brutality. A return to the heart of Fleece's sermon indicates that the scene is more than the comic relief it at first appears to be. Addressing the gluttonous sharks, Fleece really delivers an ironic thrust at Stubb, who, at the same time, is stuffing himself with whale meat:

"Your woraciousness, fellow-critters, I don't blame ye so much for; dat is natur, and can't be helped; but to gobern dat wicket natur, dat is de pint. You is sharks, sartin; but if you gobern de shark in you, why den you be angel; for all angel is not'ing more dan de shark well goberned. Now, look here, bred'ren, just try wonst to be cibil, a-helping yourselbs from dat whale. Don't be tearin' de blubber out your neighbour's mout, I say. Is not one shark dood right as toder to dat whale? And, by Gor, none on you has de right to dat whale; dat whale beong to someone else. I know some o' you has berry brig mout, brigger dan oders; but den de brig mouts sometimes has de small bellies; so dat de brigness ob de mout is not to swallar wid, but to bite off de blubber for de small fry ob sharks, dat can't get into de scrouge to help themselves." [VIII, 16]

Although Stubb does not realize as much, Fleece repays the barbs in full, for every word directed to the sharks applies as well to the sadistic mate. As Vincent aptly puts it, "Stubb's banquet and the shark's feast are ironic commentaries on each other, a grotesque antiphonal,"[30] and "While the cook preaches on the Golden Rule to the sharks, Stubb pays no attention to its meaning to himself. . . . Stubb with all his gluttonous brutality is a revelation of the evil at the heart of man."[31] With such an interlocutor, one is more inclined to pity than to laugh at the end man. Or perhaps it is Stubb who deserves the reader's pity, for in his overbearing, tasteless treatment of Fleece, he reveals a savage mentality one might expect to but does not find in the pagan harpooneers. Significantly, too, Melville gives Fleece the final word in the scene. After being forced to bow before Stubb, Fleece exits, muttering what Ishmael calls a "sage ejaculation": "Wish, by Gor! whale eat him, 'stead of him eat whale. I'm bressed if he ain't more of shark dan Massa Shark hisself" (VIII, 20).

In this way Fleece, despite his "shambling" servility and his darky dialect, offers a significant commentary on white racism. Stubb is the malicious equivalent of the "boobies and bumpkins" on the Nantucket packet, with, of course, the license of authority. Like the overseer of *Mardi,* too, but using a verbal instead of a leather lash, Stubb attempts to reduce Fleece to a dumb brute. And, to paraphrase Ishmael, he is certainly no more dignified than a whitewashed Fleece. If the Queequeg-Ishmael union is a moving example of what race relations could be, the Fleece-Stubb episode indicates what they should not be. Further, both this episode and the Daggoo-Spaniard fight underscore the basic cause of racial discord—the white man's insistence on seeing the black, not as a man, but as a subhuman figure. Fleece basically may be a "stage nigger," but he indirectly reinforces the lesson of Ishmael and Queequeg. Although Stubb would not concur, Fleece also deserves a place under the "just Spirit of Equality."

Finally, we arrive at "the most insignificant of the *Pequod's* crew"—"Black Little Pip," the "Poor Alabama boy" despised for his cowardice aboard the ship but destined to "beat his tambourine in glory" in a heaven that will hail him as a hero.

In the first extended description of Pip, Ishmael cites the traits and repeats the conventional generalizations which stamp the cabin boy as another darky stereotype:

. . . Pip, though over tender-hearted, was at bottom very bright, with that pleasant, genial, jolly brightness peculiar to his tribe; a tribe, which ever enjoy all holidays and festivities with finer, freer relish than any other race. For blacks, the year's calendar should show naught but three hundred and sixty-five Fourth of Julys and New Year's Days. [VIII, 165–166]

This observation, combined with Pip's leading the men in jigging and singing, suggests a formulaic repetition of the

Sunshine, May Day, Rose-Water presences—laughing, good-
natured souls whose main function, as far as the white man
is concerned, is to be rhythmical. Pip first appears in the
chapter entitled "Midnight, Forecastle," a chapter focusing
on the men's carousing, Daggoo's fight, and the night squall.
From the onset Pip has value to the men only so far as he
entertains them; otherwise, they regard him with contempt.
Calling for a sailor's jig, a Frenchman shouts to the boy,
"Pip! little Pip! hurrah with your tambourine!" But when
Pip plays hard-to-get—"Don't know where it is"—the Frenchman spits out, "Beat thy belly, then, and wag thy ears" (VII,
215). When he does play, they clearly delight in him: "Go it,
Pip!" and "Hold up thy hoop, Pip, till I jump through it!"
(VII, 217). The scorn, however, is ever present; when Pip
breaks one of the jinglers on the tambourine, a sailor shouts,
"Rattle thy teeth, then, and pound away; make a pagoda of
thyself" (VII, 217). To the men, Pip's position is clear; except
for the merrymaking he occasionally provides, he is, as Tashtego calls him, "a poltroon." The disdain and amused contempt with which Melville's white seamen frequently regard
the nonwhites is perhaps explained by Melville himself in a
sketch entitled "The Gees": "Of all men seamen have strong
prejudices, particularly in the matter of race. They are bigots
here. But when a creature of inferior race lives among them,
an inferior tar, there seems no bound to their disdain."[32]

In a later scene during which his boat is being towed by
a harpooned whale, Pip's "insignificance" is dramatically underscored. Panic-stricken, he leaps from the boat only to find
himself choking in the line stretched taut by the stricken
whale. Stubb reluctantly orders Tashtego to cut the line,
"Damn him, cut!" And "so the whale was lost and Pip was
saved" (VIII, 167). The men assail him with "yells and exe-
crations," and Stubb caps the scene with "We can't afford to
lose whales by the likes of you; a whale would sell for thirty
times what you would, Pip, in Alabama" (VIII, 168). Stubb's
contempt for Fleece, though thinly veiled in slapstick, is thus
made overt with Pip. Despite severe warnings and threats,

Pip again leaps into the sea during the frenzy of a later chase. This time he is abandoned in favor of the whale. As Ishmael sardonically notes, ". . . Though man loved his fellow, yet man is a money-making animal, which propensity often interferes with his benevolence" (VIII, 168). In the attitudes of the men there is no "love" for the black boy, only contempt. Their leaving him a castaway, an act which destroys his sanity, extends in horribly cruel terms the significance of the Stubb-Fleece episode.

However insignificant Pip may be to the men, Melville assigns him a place high above that of the stereotype. His role is anticipated in Ishmael's admonition to the reader, "Nor smile so, while I write that this little black was brilliant, for even blackness has its brilliancy" (VIII, 166). That "brilliancy" lies, first, in his wisdom, which is "holiness" (VIII, 301). Even with his mind intact, Pip demonstrates a common sense which raises him above the frenzied crew. Cringing under the windlass during the squall which interrupted the fight between Daggoo and the Spaniard, Pip reflects on the voyage, the men involved, and Captain Ahab's hold over them:

But there they go, all cursing, and here I don't. Fine prospects to 'em; they're on the road to heaven. Hold on hard! Jimmini, what a squall! But those chaps there are worse yet—they are your white squalls, they. White squalls? white whale, shirr! shirr! Here have I heard all their chat just now, and the White Whale—shirr! shirr!—but spoken of once! and only this evening—it makes me jingle all over like my tambourine—that anaconda of an old man swore 'em in to hunt him! Oh, thou big white God aloft there somewhere in yon darkness, have mercy on this small black boy down here; preserve him from all men that have no bowels to feel fear! [VII, 221]

Notable here is his awareness of the destructive nature of Ahab's purpose. He also recognizes in the men a savagery more violent than in nature's storm. In brief, he has the sense to feel fear. And the pathos implicit in a black boy's prayer to a god he must have been taught is white marks Pip's character throughout the novel.

That pathos is dramatically realized when Stubb abandons Pip. To Ishmael, the black castaway presents a frightening image of the isolated man and a terrifying analogy to his own situation before his union with Queequeg. Ishmael notes that "the awful lonesomeness is intolerable," and, with a shudder, he continues: "The intense concentration of self in the middle of such a heartless immensity, my God! who can tell it?" (VIII, 169). Such "concentration of self" without any human support drives Pip mad, a fate that could have been Ishmael's had his "splintered heart" not been healed by Queequeg. Ishmael, we remember, is abandoned; but he is buoyed up by the coffin of his twin brother. Hence, the contrasting situations shed further light on Ishmael's salvation through a human tie. Pip has no tie; "Stubb's inexorable back was turned upon him" (VIII, 168), a brutal and final denial of Pip's humanity; alone, Pip turns "to the sun, another lonely castaway, though the loftiest and the brightest" (VIII, 168). That turn to the sun becomes, literally, a turn to his captain; Ahab is also lofty and bright, also a "lonely castaway." It is this union between the deranged cabin boy and the ungodly-godlike captain, between white man and black which, placed next to the Queequeg-Ishmael relationship, poignantly illustrates the necessity of "squeezing ourselves universally into the very milk and sperm of kindness" (VIII, 172). Significantly, these words of Ishmael appear in the chapter immediately following that in which Pip is abandoned. The juxtaposition suggests that Pip's intolerable loneliness has prompted Ishmael's call for universal kindness.

Pip's "brilliancy" lies also in his love, the "fadeless fidelity of man." He is "full of sweet things of love and gratitude" (VIII, 302). We see him softly sobbing over the encoffined Queequeg, see the "strange sweetness of his lunacy" bringing "heavenly vouchers of all our heavenly homes" (VIII, 250). Like the sick whale scorned by the French whaler, Pip is abandoned; but as the scorned whale contains valuable ambergris, so Pip houses a heart which has no price. And it is this heart which reaches out to awaken that part of Ahab long repressed—his humanity. He protects the boy from man and the gods. To the Manxman, who has seized Pip by the arm, shouting, "Peace, thou crazy loon," Ahab commands, "Hands off from that holiness!"[33] (VIII, 301). From the "frozen heavens" he shields Pip: "Here, boy; Ahab's cabin shall be Pip's home henceforth, while Ahab lives." And in the words which follow, Ahab strikes a parallel to the bond between Ishmael and Queequeg: ". . . Thou art tied to me by cords woven of my heart-strings" (VIII, 302). Significantly, Ahab chooses the same metaphor—i.e., the string or rope—which symbolically dramatizes the mutual salvation of Ishmael and Queequeg. Pip also uses the same figure; taking Ahab's hand, he says, "This seems to me, sir, as a man-rope; something that weak souls may hold by" (VIII, 302). "Monkey-rope," "heart-strings," "man-rope"—all relate to the bond of brotherhood between men of different skin colors.

Such a bond saves Ishmael and, as Pip laments, could have saved him: "Ah, now, had poor Pip but felt so kind a thing as this [Ahab's hand or "the man-rope"], perhaps he had ne'er been lost!" (VIII, 302). In turn, the bond almost saves Ahab. He tells Pip, "Thou touchest my inmost centre, boy" (VIII, 302), and, later, "There is that in thee, poor lad, which I feel too curing to my malady" (VIII, 316). To Pip's declaration, "I will never desert ye . . . sir, I must go with ye," Ahab answers, "If thou speakest thus to me much more, Ahab's purpose keels up in him" (VIII, 316). With his protective instinct and sense of humanity aroused, Ahab is nearly cured of his monomania; however, he is too thorough an Ishmael, for at the last, he orders Pip to the captain's cabin, a command leaving the restoration of Ahab's soul incomplete and leaving Pip again alone. Unlike Ishmael, Pip has nothing to sustain him; but the poor Alabama black boy brings his captain closer to the recognition acquired earlier by Ishmael, to what Tyrus Hillway calls "a recognition of his own humanity and of the need of all creatures for understanding and love."[34] Pip's love was almost Ahab's lifebuoy.

Ahab leaves Pip with a blessing, "God forever bless thee"

(VIII, 317), but a greater blessing has been the joining of their hands, "the black one with the white," an act which prompts Ahab to say, "Come! I feel prouder leading thee by thy black hand, than though I grasped an emperor's!" (VIII, 302). Somehow those clasped hands, which momentarily merge two Isolatoes into a federation of need, remain in the mind long after the Baltimores, Lavenders, and Fleeces are forgotten. Black and white, boy and man, servant and master, Pip and Ahab are also brothers under the "just Spirit of Equality."

The "kingly commons" aboard the *Pequod* form a federation which is the dramatic realization of Melville's faith in and respect for man—and above all his belief in the interconnectedness of all men, high as well as low, black as well as white. In the famous chapter "The Whiteness of the Whale" Ishmael states that the "pre-eminence" of whiteness applies "to the human race itself, giving ideal mastership over every dusky tribe" (VII, 234–35). Queequeg, Daggoo, Tashtego, Fleece, and Pip refute that "ideal." The monkey-rope which binds all men permits no "mastership," only mutual dependence.

7.   *PIERRE* AND *ISRAEL POTTER*

> *... intrepid, unprincipled, reckless, predatory,*
> *with boundless ambition, civilized in externals*
> *but a savage at heart, America is, or may yet*
> *be, the Paul Jones of nations.*

Writing to Sophia Hawthorne (January 8, 1852), Melville
was genuinely grateful for the woman's warm response to
Moby-Dick, "for as a general thing, women have small taste
for the sea."[1] Appreciative of her discerning the "allegoric
construction" of his sea saga, Melville then promised different
literary fare: "But, my Dear Lady, I shall not again send you a
bowl of salt water. The next chalice I shall commend, will be a
rural bowl of milk."[2] The "rural bowl"[3] was his seventh book,
Pierre. For the first time in his literary career Melville becomes
landlocked, setting his hero Pierre Glendinning first amid the
luxuriant surroundings of a country estate named Saddle
Meadows, then moving him to the teeming warehouse district
of a large city. This return to land and, specifically, to
America was perhaps an attempt to recapture an audience
whose reading tastes were inclined toward domestic romance.
Such a motive is apparent in Melville's description of the book
to his London publisher Richard Bentley as a work "treating

of utterly new scenes and characters;—and, as I believe, very much more calculated for popularity than anything you have yet published of mine—being a regular romance, with a mysterious plot to it & stirring passions at work, and withall, representing a new & elevated aspect of American life."[4]

This work of "unquestionable novelty" is the first in Melville's canon in which all the characters are white. As to the absence of nonwhites, one can only speculate. Perhaps the sea is the key. Melville's seagoing narrators—Tommo, Taji, Redburn, White-Jacket, and Ishmael—generally respond to their fellow mariners, dark or white, with tolerance, sympathy, and occasionally respect. Away from the insular prejudices of civilized men, they learn, as does Huck Finn aboard the raft, to judge men, not as society conveniently stereotypes races and nationalities, but as human beings. Possibly, racial harmony was a subject Melville could comfortably explore only on an island remote from civilization or on a ship at sea. Of course, such a conjecture should not rule out the obvious reason behind the absence of nonwhites in *Pierre*—that a romance dealing with "stirring passions" and lacking masculine camaraderie and adventure (except for the philosophical adventures of the mind) simply had no reason for including dusky-skinned savages and proud or servile Negroes. In short, Melville in *Pierre* is concerned, not with the relationships among men, but with "the truth of the human heart," which Hawthorne indicated is central to a good romance. Melville's seventh book, then, probably should not enter into an examination of his nonwhite characters; yet *Pierre* does yield some interesting echoes of themes associated with Melville's nonwhites. The echoes may be faint, but they deserve brief consideration.

In his sketch of Pierre's grandfather, old Pierre Glendinning, Melville indirectly illuminates the savagery which seems inherent in some of the nonwhites discussed earlier. Old Pierre is "the mildest hearted, and most blue-eyed gentleman in the world," "a forgiver of many injuries; a sweet-hearted, charitable Christian; in fine, a pure, cheerful, childlike, . . . divine old man."[5] At the same time, this robust man of "substantial person" is a grand warrior, a revolutionary war hero who, on one occasion, "annihilated two Indian savages by making reciprocal bludgeons of their heads" (pp. 29–30). Sweet and savage, meek and stern, Christian and warlike—General Glendinning's character derives from the duality associated with Melville's South Sea natives and some of the seagoing blacks. In fact, old Pierre seems a refined, Americanized Typee. Even more notable is how easily his sketch could describe Queequeg. Both are "cheerful," "charitable," and "mild-hearted"; both are capable of annihilating an enemy. Here, Melville sees that duality in a positive light, suggesting that it may be a condition natural to noble men: the general's soul is both "meek" and "majestic"; in it "the lion and the lamb embraced—fit image of his God" (p. 30). Again, this time with a white warrior, Melville sees man as God's image; interestingly enough, that image evokes respect and admiration for its balance of meekness and majesty. The characters lacking the balance of lion and lamb, it should be recalled, are soulless. Witness, for example, Landless in *White-Jacket,* who is "without a soul" because he responds to humiliation with indifference. The overseer in *Mardi* sees the tribe of Hamo as "soulless." And old Baltimore, though treated sympathetically by Melville, is "too good natured"—too much a lamb. He lacks "the temper of a wolf." Not to ignore the other extreme, one might add here Bembo and Stubb as being too much "wolf" or "shark." The right condition, the ideal soul, requires both the humanity of the Christian and the fierceness of the savage. Certainly in Queequeg's soul the lion and lamb embrace. White Glendinning and brown Queequeg, ideally balanced images of God, offer further evidence of Melville's indifference to skin color as a measure of man's worth. In Melville's estimate of the individual, what matters is the quality of the soul.

General Glendinning, brief as his portrait may be, is also the third slaveowner to appear in Melville's fiction. In summarizing the old warrior's virtues, the narrator calls him "the kindest of masters to his slaves" (p. 30). This observation,

included in a sentence which also notes the man's devotion to
his wife and children—"the gentlest husband, and the gentlest
father"—emphasizes a warm fatherly relationship. Into that
relationship we are permitted only brief glimpses. We know,
for example, that the general, a great lover of horses, trusted
their care to only one person besides himself, Moyer, "an
incorruptible and most punctual old black" (p. 30). In a
sense, granting such an "honourable office" to Moyer is granting trust and respect. Glendinning's treatment of his slaves
recalls White-Jacket's cherishing "an involuntary friendliness"
toward the purser for "his pleasant, kind, indulgent manner
toward his slave" (p. 379). In a word, both owners treat the
blacks as humans. In this connection, it is interesting to note
the punishment old Pierre reserves for his blacks if they should
leave a horse unblanketed or unfed. He would not have them
flogged; "but he would refuse to say his wonted pleasant word
to them; and that was very bitter to them, for . . . [they] loved
grand old Pierre, as his shepherds loved old Abraham" (p.
30). Like the purser, old Pierre replaces the severity of the
lash with a punishment which recognizes the slaves' capacity
to feel. Again, we sense Melville's approval of the white man
who refuses to brutalize the black—who, in short, recognizes
the black's essential humanity.

Pierre also contains an observation on humor which may
indirectly account for Melville's employing some dark-skinned
characters as objects of laughter. After satirizing an assorted
group of artists and philosophers who "strive to make ample
amends for their physical forlornness, by resolutely revelling in
the region of blissful ideals," Melville honors them as "noble
men often at bottom." He then adds, "And for that very reason
I make bold to be gamesome about them; for where fundamental nobleness is, and fundamental honour is due, merri-
ment is never accounted irreverent" (p. 267). It is tempting
to reconsider Melville's comic treatment of figures such as
Baltimore and Old Coffee in the light of this observation. This
study has conceded Melville's tendency to be "gamesome" with
his darkies; at the same time, it has been pointed out that

through the minstrel-show trappings characterizing such figures, Melville's sympathy or respect, and occasionally both, are apparent. Considering Melville's emphasis throughout his fiction on the fundamental dignity of man, it is difficult to see disrespect in his jests. He intends no offense, no irreverence with his laughter, because he acknowledges the "fundamental honour" of all men. His laughter carries with it the warmth and good nature which characterizes friendly teasing. It is laughter marked by tenderness, and, as such, it does not debase. Melville's good-natured joshing of Baltimore contrasted with Stubb's treatment of Fleece dramatically underscores the difference between laughter free from malice and laughter intended to degrade. As for those who would take offense at Melville's "gamesome" treatment of nonwhites, perhaps Melville himself provides the most appropriate answer: "The fools and pretenders of humanity, and the imposters and baboons among the gods, these only are offended with raillery" (pp. 267–68).

Since *Pierre* contains only white characters, it is only peripheral to a study devoted to nonwhite figures; admittedly, Melville's attitude toward old Pierre Glendinning and his comment on humor should not be wrenched out of context and applied to characters in other books. Nonetheless, the above facets of *Pierre* do echo thematic considerations associated with Melville's handling of nonwhite characters and, in so doing, indicate a consistent attitude on Melville's part.

Melville's eighth full-length work was *Israel Potter* (1855).[6] In offering the work to Putnam's, he promised a book that "shall contain nothing of any sort to shock the fastidious. There will be very little reflective writing in it; nothing weighty. It is adventure."[7] Adventurous it is. From Bunker Hill to the battle beween the *Bon Homme Richard* and the *Serapis,* the hero Israel Potter, as soldier, sailor, and spy, manages to meet such notables as King George III, Horne Tooke, Ben Franklin, John Paul Jones, and Ethan Allen. The last three, though somewhat flat as characters, appear not just for the magic of their presence; through them Melville seems to be reflecting

on the American national character. Of special interest to this
study are the portraits of John Paul Jones and Ethan Allen.
As was the case with *Pierre, Israel Potter* contains only white
characters; yet both Jones and Allen offer intriguing parallels
to some of Melville's nonwhites, especially the dusky savages
of the South Pacific.

As Melville depicts him, John Paul Jones is an impressive
figure. Intrepid, proud, gallant, humane—all are apt adjectives
in his portrait. Melville calls him a "citizen of the universe"
and "an extraordinary warrior." Significantly, this "devil in a
Scotch bonnet" is "extraordinary" because of the "apparent
incompatibilities" of "regicidal daring" and "octogenarian pru-
dence."[8] This paradox echoes the lion-lamb, savage-Christian
combination which Melville's most memorable and admirable
characters possess. In this connection his resemblance to Melville's dusky Polynesians is unmistakable. Consistently he is
compared to nonwhites. Twice his complexion is described as
"tawny," a color which "spoke of the tropic." He has a "savage,
self-possessed eye" and "a grim and Feejee air." Jones refers
to himself as "a bloody cannibal." The most obvious link to
the Polynesian savage is the tattoo on his arm, a design of
"large intertwisted ciphers . . . wholly unlike the fanciful
figures of anchors, hearts, and cables, sometimes decorating
small portions of seamen's bodies. It was a sort of tattooing
such as is seen only on thorough-bred savages—deep blue,
elaborate, labyrinthine, cabalistic" (p.81). Israel recalls seeing
a similar design on the arm of a New Zealand warrior. Jones
is also associated with the American Indian. His aspect is that
"of a disinherited Indian chief in European clothes." He is
like "a prowling *brave*." In battle he waves his hand "like a
disdainful tomahawk." He is erect, "like an Iroquois," and has
the "look . . . of a parading Sioux demanding homage to his
gewgaws." Reinforcing these images is Jones's character. Like
Queequeg and Daggoo, "He looked like one who never had
been, and never would be a subordinate" (p. 72). Proud and
defiant, like Bembo, Samoa, and other vindictive nonwhites,
he is quickly triggered into action by the motive of revenge.

His argument for receiving a commission, for example, is to teach the British "that if they ruthlessly ravage the American coasts, their own coasts are vulnerable as New Holland's" (p. 73). Also, his raid on Whitehaven is an act of vengeance on a people who, he believes, slandered him. Still another similarity to Melville's dusky barbarians should be noted: he has about him a "cool solemnity" which recalls the self-possession of Queequeg, Tashtego, and the Typees. His actions during the encounter with the *Drake* are marked by the same aplomb which characterizes Queequeg's conflict with the greenhorn on the Nantucket packet: he gazes in "audacious tranquility" at the enemy and "amicably" returns the hail "with complete self-possession" (pp. 130–31).

The blend of savagery and self-possession—the man-devil duality implicit in Melville's savage characters throughout his earier works—is pronounced in the character of Jones. Melville even calls him "a mixture of gentleman and wolf" (p. 125). Nowhere is the duality more strongly suggested than in "the laced coat-sleeve" which covers Jones's tattooed arm and in the hand at the end of that arm—a hand "half muffled in ruffles, and ornamented with several Parisian rings" (p. 81). This incongruity prompts Melville to an observation which echoes his earlier discovery about the uncivilized man: ". . . Brooches and finger-rings, not less than nose-rings and tattooings, are tokens of the primeval savageness which ever slumbers in human kind, civilized or uncivilized" (pp. 81–82).

By attributing to a white American naval hero the same traits which mark his dark-skinned characters, Melville blurs any distinction between the civilized and uncivilized man, between the white and the dark skin. The portrait of John Paul Jones placed next to that of Queequeg underscores the sameness of man and the irrelevance of man's exterior. To paraphrase Ishmael, a man can be honest or barbaric in any kind of skin.

Israel Potter's relations with John Paul Jones end with the terrifyingly destructive engagement between the *Bon Homme Richard* and the *Serapis*. The two chapters devoted to the carnage are climaxed with a question which, from *Typee* through *Billy Budd,* represents one of Melville's major themes: "What separates the enlightened man from the savage? Is civilization a thing distinct, or is it an advanced stage of barbarism?" (p. 173). From the indictment of civilized man in *Typee* and *Omoo* to the admirable stature of Queequeg in *Moby-Dick,* Melville's answer to this question consistently stresses a concern with inner substance rather than with the outer man. *Israel Potter* reinforces this concern.

The events involving Ethan Allen show to what extent civilization is "an advanced stage of barbarism." Allen, "a martial man of Patagonian stature" (p. 189), is a Western version of Bembo—wild, ferocious, vindictive. Melville surrounds him with animal images: he roars like a "tormented lion"; his words are "bayed out"; as a captive, he seems "like some baited bull in the ring"; he has "leopard-like teeth" and a "broad, bovine forehead"; "ferocious in the last degree," he is treated by his British captors "as a lion of Asia . . . too dreadful to behold without fear and trembling, and consequent cruelty" (p. 199). But after noting that "his whole marred aspect was that of some wild beast," Melville qualifies the animalistic impression in a manner which we have seen before; if a beast, Allen was "of a royal sort, and unsubdued by the cage" (p. 191). Here we sense a familiar Melville suject—that of the man who, in attempting to preserve his essential dignity, strikes back at those who would brutalize or, in this case, encage him. Rather than condemn Allen's barbarous acts, Melville clearly justifies them. The British have treated Allen "with inexcusable cruelty and indignity; something as if he had fallen into the hands of the Dyaks" (pp. 198–99). Further, the British have "violated every international usage of right and decency, in treating a distinguished prisoner of war as if he had been a Botany Bay convict" (p. 200). These charges should answer Melville's question about whether civilization is a "thing distinct." As has been noted, Melville's response is to describe a person so treated as fighting and baiting his tormentors; submission and endurance will not salvage dignity. Accordingly, Melville justifies Allen's savagery: ". . . By assuming the part of a jocular, reckless, and even braggart barbarian, he would better sustain himself against bullying turnkeys, than by submissive quietude" (p. 200). More obvious is his terse advice—"When among wild beasts, if they menace you, be a wild beast" (p. 200).

Thus, Ethan Allen, though white, embodies characteristics which Melville frequently attributes to his nonwhite characters. Like them, he has been exasperated into savagery, in this case by a people supposedly enlightened. Through Ethan Allen, Melville once again defends savage retaliation as sometimes vital to the preservation of the dignity of man.

Old Pierre Glendinning, John Paul Jones, Ethan Allen— heroes, patriots, warriors—all are cast in the mold of Melville's dark-skinned savages. The similarities between the whites and the nonwhites confirm Melville's acknowledgment of the "common continent of men."

8. *THE CONFIDENCE-MAN*

> *. . . It should not, in self defense, be held for a reasonable maxim, that none but the good are human.*

> *. . . Where the wolves are killed off, the foxes increase.*

The Confidence-Man (1857), Melville's last and least understood novel, is set, like *Pierre,* in America. Though inland, Melville retains the familiar analogy of the ship to the world; this time the vessel is the riverboat *Fidele* churning through the heartland of America on the Mississippi, which, in "uniting the streams of the most distant and opposite zones," represents "the dashing and all-fusing spirit of the West."[1] Once again the persons aboard ship compose an Anacharsis Clootz deputation:

Natives of all sorts, and foreigners; men of business and men of pleasure; parlour men and backwoodsmen, farm-hunters and fame-hunters; heiress-hunters, gold-hunters, buffalo-hunters, bee-hunters, happiness-hunters, truth-hunters, and still keener hunters after all these hunters. Fine ladies in slippers, and moccasined squaws; Northern speculators and Eastern philosophers; English, Irish, German, Scotch, Danes; Santa Fe traders in striped blankets, and Broadway bucks in cravats of cloth of gold; fine-looking Missis-

. sippi cotton-planters; Quakers in full drab, and United States
soldiers in full regimentals; slaves, black, mulatto, quadroon; mod-
ish young Spanish Creoles, and old-fashioned French Jews; Mor-
mons and Papists; Dives and Lazarus; jesters and mourners,
teetotalers and convivialists, deacons and blacklegs; hard-shell
Baptists and clay-eaters; grinning negroes, and Sioux chiefs solemn
as high priests. In short, a piebald parliament, an Anacharsis
Cloots congress of all kinds of that multiform pilgrim species, man.
[Pp. 8–9]

This analogy, vital to *Moby-Dick* and included later in *Billy
Budd,* must have been central to Melville's conception of the
world. Its recurrence underscores what this study has attempted to show—Melville's belief in the sameness of man,
his view that, regardless of race or national origin, "we are all
good and bad."[2] In *The Confidence-Man,* however, the Anacharsis Clootz analogy hardly signals an optimistic faith in
the harmonious interconnectedness of all men. Through the
confidence man, who dons various disguises to bilk the river-
boat passengers, Melville creates a bleak vision of human life
as an intricate con game. The "piebald parliament" on the
Fidele, unlike the "kingly commons" on the *Pequod,* is a
collection of frauds and shams. If, as the novel repeatedly
shows, human goodness, benevolence, and trust are but traps
for man, who is depicted as hypocritical, avaricious, and
stupid, then Melville's "monkey-rope" may appropriately
become a universal gallows.

No critical dexterity is necessary to see the book's negation; in this respect, readers are fairly unanimous. Chase
calls it "a disillusioned and savage book";[3] Arvin, "one of the
most *infidel* books ever written by an American; one of the
most completely nihilistic, morally and metaphysically";[4]
Mumford, "an indictment of humanity . . . far more deeply
corrosive than anything in Bierce or Mark Twain";[5] William
Braswell, a book containing "Melville's most cynical views on
man."[6] Even those who see the work as high comedy, e.g.,
Howard[7] and Franklin,[8] are quick to note the aftertaste of
bitterness. The most intriguing problem in *The Confidence-
Man* centers on the state of the mind which produced such a

despairing account of man. But, as noted, Melville's belief in the sameness of man, however deplorable man's state may be, is yet evident in this last novel. His depiction of and comments on nonwhites in *The Confidence-Man* emphasize the Anacharsis Clootz analogy; this time, however, the "congress" of man is riddled by distrust: ". . . Did you never observe how little, very little, confidence, there is? I mean between man and man—more particularly between stranger and stranger. In a sad world it is the saddest fact" (p. 34).

One nonwhite appears in *The Confidence-Man,* a crippled Negro beggar named Guinea. He is the second mask assumed by the confidence man. The first is a flaxen-haired stranger in cream-colors who writes a message of faith, hope, and charity on a slate, is scorned by the passengers aboard the *Fidele,* falls asleep in "lamblike" innocence, and then departs unnoticed. Few readers of Melville doubt that this "lamblike" man recently arrived from the East is a Christ figure, but there is disagreement over his specific role. Some critics see him as a false Christ, the first avatar of the confidence man.[9] Others contend that he is a benevolent Christ and, as such, a contrast to the "devilish" Black Guinea, John W. Shroeder, for example, notes "a certain ominous quality in this Negro; he may be an inhabitant of the fiery pit."[10] James E. Miller, Jr., also sees Guinea as the Devil, contrasting with the lamblike man who is Christ.[11] Whether or not Guinea is the "Black Man," as the Calvinists repeatedly represented Satan, the reader may judge for himself. One thing seems clear; although Black Guinea is somehow related to the confidence man, the clues to his identity are few. Perhaps it would be most useful to examine him simply as a Negro character and not as one of the roles assumed by the confidence man.

On the surface, Guinea faintly echoes Melville's black sea-cooks, but there is no humor attached to this "grotesque negro cripple." He is a servile, grinning object of cruel amusement. As the animal images surrounding him suggest, Guinea is dehumanized. On his stunted legs, which reduce him "to the stature of a Newfoundland dog," he shufflles about, rubbing

his face "against the upper part of people's thighs." His
bushy wool resembles "the curled forehead of a black steer."
He is "like a half-frozen black sheep nudging itself a cozy
berth in the heart of the white flock." As he begs for pennies,
we see him "throwing back his head and opening his mouth
like an elephant for tossed apples at a menagerie." Finally
Guinea refers to himself as "der dog widout massa." The
portrait is hardly one deserving of respect; stripped of his
manhood, the character repels. Also evident in his portrait
are the conventional trappings of the Negro as merrymaker.
Equipped with the standard tambourine, he makes even "the
gravest" smile. Melville continues, "It was curious to see him,
out of his very deformity, indigence, and houselessness, so
cheerily endured, raising mirth in some of that crowd, whose
own purses, hearths, hearts, all their possessions, sound limbs
included, could not make gay" (p. 10). As was the case with
Pip, and to a lesser degree with Sunshine, May Day, and
Rose-Water, Guinea's function, as far as the white passengers
are concerned, is to be entertaining. He is a dog to be petted
or kicked and a servile end man to be laughed at.

Guinea's relationship with the whites offers Melville
another opportunity to indict white civilized man. Perhaps the
most painful image of Guinea is his role in the "pitch-penny"
game, his "mouth being at once target and purse" (p. 12) for
the coppers tossed by the amused crowd. Swallowing any
emotion he may feel, he grins; but the grin becomes a "wince"
when some of the almsgivers substitute buttons for pennies
and bounce them off his teeth. This "game of charity" is
reminiscent of the Stubb-Fleece episode in *Moby-Dick* and
offers a similar indictment. Guinea, even more than Fleece,
is a pitiful figure, a creature to be abused for one's amusement, something subhuman rather than a man; like Fleece,
his subhuman status results from the tasteless treatment he
receives at the hands of the whites. Like spectators tossing
peanuts to and at encaged animals, the passengers seem
more deserving of pity than does the brute. Like Stubb,
Mardi's overseer, and Captain Claret, the whites readily

accept and perpetuate the image of the Negro as an animal. The scene is also thematically significant. Just as the passengers scorned the message of charity from the lamblike man, here they make charity a cruel, dehumanizing game. Their treatment of Guinea is an ironic thrust at one of the lamblike man's messages: *Charity suffereth long, and is kind.* The kindness here is the kindness of the shark. It is tempting to apply to Guinea White-Jacket's lament for Rose-Water: "Heaven send you a release from your humiliation." To do so, however, is to ignore another possibility: Black Guinea is not blameless. He initiates the pitch-penny game because the passengers, "used at last to his strange looks . . . began to get their fill of him as a curious object" (p. 11). His game revives their interest, and Melville suggests that their response is warranted: "As in appearance he seemed a dog, so now, in a merry way, like a dog he began to be treated" (p. 11). Again Melville has demonstrated that servility and submission earn only indignity. Guinea then can be added to the non-white characters who, though deserving of pity and sympathy, do not earn respect. That is due those who, like Daggoo, Queequeg, Samoa, and even Bembo, neither cringe nor fawn. Guinea needs to learn the lesson of Ethan Allen: by assuming the part of the savage "he would better sustain himself against bullying turnkeys, than by submissive quietude."[12] Perhaps if he were less the "lamb" and more the "lion," he would attain the kind of balance which marks a man. All we can say with any certainty is that Guinea's role, his acceptance of being abused while deserving that abuse, reflects what the novel accomplishes—the undermining of our assurances about the proper object of our pity and respect.

Complicating the reader's response to Guinea is the possibility that he is a white man impersonating a black, one of the masks assumed with such slick dexterity by the confidence man. But who or what is the confidence man? Is he, as Hennig Cohen suggests, "a supernatural being of some kind in a variety of incarnations"?[13] Is he, as Chase reads him, a composite figure of folklore, the embodiment of the Yankee

peddler and the Westerner?[14] A cynical cripple aboard the
Fidele, who to some critics is Melville's spokesman, dismisses
Guinea as a fake, a "white operator betwisted and painted
up for a decoy" (p. 15). If the cynical man is right, and he
defends his accusation by pointing to the ease with which
white men become Negroes in minstrel shows, then we have
another example of a white character who automatically
stereotypes the black man. It is significant that the white man
masquerading as a Negro makes dominant in his masquerade
the stock characteristics: the grin, the plaintive wail, the
good-natured face, the doglike fawning. In short, to the white
man the Negro is a formula. Later, the confidence man in
another role (agent of the Black Rapids Coal Company)
chances to speak of Negroes, and his generalizations about the
race confirm his earlier impersonation of Guinea:

". . . Negroes were by nature a singularly cheerful race; no one
ever head of a native-born African Zimmerman or Torquemada;
. . . even from religion they dismissed all gloom; in their hilarious
rituals they danced, so to speak, and, as it were, cut pigeon-wings.
It was improbable, therefore, that a negro, however reduced to his
stumps by fortune, could be ever thrown off the legs of a laughing
philosophy." [Pp. 75–76]

His stereotyped description of the race parallels his stereotyped portrayal of one of its members.[15] One who is accustomed to reducing the Negro to a formula when impersonating the black man could hardly be expected to invest him
with any traits of humanity. Once again we wonder whether
Melville is degrading the black through stereotype or whether
he is indicting the white man for his oversimplification of the
black character. In this respect, Franklin's observation on the
novel seems appropriate: "Confidence and distrust, tame animals and wild animals—all become indistinguishable in a
universe in which black is only another appearance of
white."[16] If Black Guinea is "only another appearance" of the
white man, then Melville again has demonstrated, cynically
this time, the universal sameness of man.

Before we leave Guinea, it should be noted that his role

in the novel, though small, is important. As they become suspicious of Guinea, lacking confidence in him and refusing him charity, the passengers insist that he produce someone to vouch for him. Guinea responds with a list of men who subsequently become masks donned by the confidence man. His list is basic to the book's structure. As Edward H. Rosenberry has noted, "In every way this initial episode concerning the veracity of the Negro beggar Black Guinea is a key to all that follows. It sets the dramatic pattern, it lists the principal characters or disguises to follow and it states the theme of the action."[17]

Like the shape-shifting confidence man himself, in fact, like the entire novel, Guinea is an elusive character. The reader is confronted with complexities and contradictions not easily reconciled. Matthiessen's note that, by having the characters disembark, Melville "could dodge the necessity of sustaining the implications of any of them,"[18] applies all too well to Guinea, for his part is marked by implications. He is a grinning darky, a deserving object of the white man's abuse; as a white man assuming the stereotyped characteristics of the darky, he is an indirect criticism of the whites who see the Negro as a formula; his treatment by the whites, who deny him charity and trust, dramatically illustrates the negative view of man advanced by the book. To some extent, all of these implications echo themes associated with the nonwhite characters in Melville's earlier books. But before we conveniently categorize Guinea, it would be well to remember that we are dealing with the confidence man—who on one occasion warns, "You can conclude nothing absolute from the human form" (p. 300). To reach an "absolute conclusion" about Black Guinea may be to play into the hands of the confidence man, who would have us believe that black is distinguishable from white.

No other nonwhite characters appear in *The Confidence-Man,* but the Indian and his relationship with the backwoodsman occupy the center of a conversation between Charles Arnold Noble and the confidence man in the guise of "the

cosmopolitan." Overhearing a discussion between the cosmopolitan and a frontiersman dressed in buckskin, Noble is
reminded of the misanthropy of Colonel John Moredock of
Illinois, the Indian-hater. But to make Moredock's career
more comprehensible, he first explains to the cosmopolitan
the "Metaphysics of Indian-Hating" as related by his father's
friend Judge James Hall.[19] In the account of the Indian-hater
generally and of Moredock's career specifically, the Indian is
depicted in a searingly negative light. As such, the portrait is
drastically inconsistent with the image of the nonwhite throughout Melville's fiction.

In the "Metaphysics of Indian-Hating" the judge advances
the backwoodsman's impression of Indians; the result is an
abhorrent picture of an entire race. All his generalizations
about the Indian blend into the cliché, "The only good Indian
is a dead one." In his education, for example, the backwoodsman hears "little from his schoolmasters . . . but histories of
Indian lying, Indian theft, Indian double-dealing, Indian
fraud and perfidy, Indian want of conscience, Indian blood-
thirstiness, Indian diabolism—histories which, though of wild
woods, are almost as full of things unangelic as the Newgate
Calendar or the Annals of Europe" (pp. 194–95). Even the
Indian converted to Christianity, the judge avers, will not
conceal his conviction "that his race's portion by nature is
total depravity" (p. 196). As for "kind" Indians, they are
"mostly lazy, and reputed simple—at all events, are seldom
chiefs," and they "may be forced to do unkind biddings"
(p. 198). And the "friendly" Indian "is a very rare sort of
creature; and well it was so, for no ruthlessness exceeds that
of a 'friendly Indian' turned enemy. A coward friend, he
makes a valiant foe" (p. 199). In short, the backwoodsman
(and, one suspects, the judge) regards the Indian "in much
the same spirit that a jury does a murderer, or a trapper a
wildcat—a creature in whose behalf mercy were not wisdom;
truce is vain; he must be executed" (p. 192). The generalizations show again the white man stereotyping and, in so doing,
stripping the nonwhite of any sense of humanity. Seeing the

nonwhite as a subhuman figure, the white plants the seeds of racial strife.

Interestingly enough, some readers see in Judge Hall's view of the Indian Melville's indirect denunciation of a race. Hennig Cohen, for one, notes that Melville "takes pains to have his narrator portray him [the Indian] as a diabolical monster who, like the confidence-man, is an arch dissembler."[20] In his analysis of the figurative language in the book, John W. Shroeder goes further, stating that "hatred of the snake amounts to positive virtue in the cosmos of the *Fidele*. And the Indian . . . is coupled with the serpent in no accidental fashion."[21] Noting that the novel offers "a running system of Indian-images related to concepts, situations, and persons connected with the theological doctrines of human guilt and damnation,"[22] Shroeder argues that the only remedy against the confidence man is the Indian-hater.[23] If correct, such readers attribute to Melville a racial attitude nowhere evident in his other work—an attitude, it would appear, which appropriately concurs with the "bitter and depressed" Melville of the 1850s. But aside from taking Judge Hall's attitudes as Melville's, such a view fails to note the quality of the man who has made Indian-hating his religion. As Roy Harvey Pearce cogently argues, viewing the Indians as satanic "depends finally upon demonstrating the justness of the Indian-hater's attitude toward them. Without that demonstration, such references [i.e., to the serpent and Satan] can be taken to point simply to Indians as natural men, who are good and evil in the way in which nature is good and evil."[24] Let us examine, then, the backwoodsman as the narrator portrays him:

The backwoodsman is a lonely man. He is a thoughtful man. He is a man strong and unsophisticated. Impulsive, he is what some might call unprincipled. At any rate he is self-willed. . . . he must depend upon himself; he must continually look to himself. Hence self reliance, to the degree of standing by his own judgment, though it stand alone. Not that he deems himself infallible . . . but he thinks that nature destines such sagacity as she has given him, as she destines it to the 'possum. . . . Like the 'possum, the backwoodsman presents the spectacle of a creature dwelling ex-

clusively among the works of God, yet these, truth must confess,
breed little in him of a godly mind. . . . The sight of smoke ten
miles off is provocation to one more remove from man, one step
deeper into nature. Is it that he feels that whatever many may be,
man is not the universe? . . . Be that how it will, the backwoodsman is not without some fineness to his nature. Hairy Orson as
he looks, it may be with him as with the Shetland seal—beneath
the bristles lurks the fur.

Though held . . . a sort of barbarian, the backwoodsman would
seem to America what Alexander was to Asia—captain in the
vanguard of conquering civilization. [Pp. 192–93]

The description is revealing. The last sentence immediately
reminds us of Melville's attitude toward "conquering civilization," of his indictment of civilized man in *Typee* and *Omoo,*
and of the respect and admiration he shows for those nonwhites not dehumanized by civilization. "Captain of conquering civilization" is no more a complimentary title in *The
Confidence-Man* than it was in those first two books, for our
backwoodsman "captain" becomes indistinguishable from the
savagery he would conquer. He is "a creature," "a 'possum"
relying on instinct, a beast beneath whose "bristles lurks the
fur." With "little in him of a godly mind," he is an Isolato
who, in seceding from the common continent of men,[25] becomes a savage or, more accurately, a "snuffing" and "smell-
ing" animal implacably and blindly dedicated to vengeance.

As for Colonel Moredock, his vengeance would appear
justified, for his family had been slaughtered by "a band of
twenty renegades from various tribes, outlaws even among
Indians . . . who had formed themselves into a marauding
crew" (p. 204). But Moredock is not content to avenge himself on this "gang of Cains" (p. 205). For the crimes committed by twenty outcasts of a race, he makes exterminating
the entire race his passion. "Never let[ting] pass an opportunity of quenching an Indian" (p. 206), Moredock becomes
a slave to that passion. In this parable of racial hatred the
colonel is dehumanized, seeing, as Pearce notes, "nothing but
the dark side of life. In that darkness he loses sight of his
human self."[26] Daniel Hoffman, too, sees Moredock's commitment to revenge as a "sterile, mechanical defeat of all his

human promise."[27] Moredock's career of barbarity and remorseless cruelty places him on the same level as the "gang
of Cains" which provoked his revenge. He, too, is a Cain—
hardly a hero. As Pearce says, "Melville has no more praise
for Indian-hating than he does for confidence. Both are false,
blind, unreasoning."[28]

If the Indian in *The Confidence-Man* is portrayed as a
beast and a diabolical savage, that portrait is done by a beast
who would implacably "abhor an entire race" (p. 195).
Melville is not really making the "captain of conquering civilization" a hero. In fact, Melville's implicit condemnation of
the Indian-hater is consistent with his defense of the Indian
in his review in the *Literary World* (March 31, 1849) of
Parkman's *Oregon Trail*. That defense is worth citing in full:

> . . . When in the body of the book we are informed that it is diffi-
> cult for any white man, after a domestication among the Indians,
> to hold them much better than brutes; when we are told, too, that
> to such a person, the slaughter of an Indian is indifferent as the
> slaughter of a buffalo; with all deference, we beg leave to dissent.
> It is too often the case, that civilized beings sojourning among
> savages soon come to regard them with disdain and contempt. But
> though in many cases this feeling is almost natural, it is not de-
> fensible; and it is wholly wrong. Why should we contemn them?
> Because we are better than they? Assuredly not. . . . When we
> affect to contemn savages, we should remember that by so doing
> we asperse our own progenitors; for they were savages also. Who
> can swear, that among the naked British barbarians sent to Rome
> to be stared at more than 1500 years ago, the ancestor of Bacon
> might not have been found? Why, among the very Thugs of India,
> or the bloody Dyaks of Borneo, exists the germ of all that is in-
> tellectually elevated and grand. We are all of us—Anglo-Saxons,
> Dyaks, and Indians—sprung from one head, and made in one
> image. And if we regret this brotherhood now, we shall be forced
> to join hands hereafter. A misfortune is not a fault; and good luck
> is not meritorious. The savage is born a savage; and the civilized
> being but inherits his civilization, nothing more.[29]

Melville's corrosive indictment of humanity in *The Confidence-Man* stands in stark contrast to his faith in the "kingly
commons" of *Moby-Dick*. The fact remains, however, that
his treatment of the nonwhite in the person of Black Guinea
and his response to race relations in the Indian-hater chapters

are consistent with his attitudes toward these subjects throughout his fiction. To be sure, the perspective is different. Or is it? Perhaps Sedgwick is right when he concludes from the Indian-hater episode: "The man of hate is the man of love. He hates precisely because he loves. The angry satirist and not the man who blandly dismisses him is the true believer in his kind."[30] Whether Melville hates or loves, *The Confidence-Man* reinforces his emphasis on the sameness of man.

9. *BENITO CERENO*

*"So far may even the best man err, in judging
the conduct of one with the recesses of whose
condition he is not acquainted. But you were
forced to it; and you were in time undeceived.
Would that, in both respects, it was so ever,
and with all men."*

Benito Cereno, Melville's tale of mutiny aboard the Spanish
ship *San Dominick* captained by Don Benito Cereno, is a
drama in which nonwhites occupy center stage. The story
unfolds through the consciousness of a native of Duxbury,
Massachusetts, Captain Amasa Delano, who, seeing the *San
Dominick* in a shocking state of decay floundering toward a
reef, comes to its aid. Once aboard, Delano cannot know
what Benito does—that the principal cargo of the vessel, 160
Negro slaves, have mutinied and killed most of the crew.
Their leader is the Senegalese Negro Babo, who, disguised as
the solicitous body servant of Cereno, has organized every
person aboard in an ingenious masquerade to deceive the
American captain. Alternating between mistrust and reas-
surance over the ambiguous actions of Cereno, crew and
slaves, but failing to penetrate the true nature of the mystery,
Delano's mind makes *Benito Cereno* a masterpiece of sus-

pense, many particulars of which are not known until after the narrative climax. At this point, the specifics of the revolt are revealed through lengthy extracts from the testimony of Benito, who gives his deposition during the trial of the mutineers. Suspense, however, is of secondary importance. The fascinating enigma of *Benito Cereno* revolves around the question of what Melville intended his blacks to be.

Black is evil. In this direction leans one school of critics, who, with some variation, subscribe to Charles Neider's view that "Melville glosses over extenuating circumstances in an effort to blacken the blacks and whiten the whites, to create poetic images of pure evil and pure virtue."[1] Arvin sees the Negroes as "monsters who persecute or tyrannize,"[2] and Babo as "a monster out of Gothic fiction at its worst."[3] Franklin calls the Negroes "a malignant destructive force,"[4] embodying "savage terror and naked evil."[5] Howard suggests that the source of *Benito Cereno,* Captain Amasa Delano's *Narrative of Voyages and Travels,* appealed to Melville because "it made the 'darkness' of life visible in the primitive blacks."[6] Comparing the tale with the source, Howard says that Babo was transformed from the original and "made the evil genius of the entire story."[7] Working with the source before Howard did, Rosalie Feltenstein argues that Melville "elevates the character of Benito Cereno" and "turns Babo into a manifestation of pure evil."[8] Many critics speak of Babo in terms of "motiveless malignity" and compare him to Iago. Generally, those readers interpreting the Negro as the embodiment of evil cite as evidence Melville's alteration of the source, the atrocities committed by the blacks, and the animal images surrounding them; and in response to critics such as Matthiessen, who says, "Although the Negroes were savagely vindictive . . . the fact remains that they were slaves and that evil had thus originally been done to them,"[9] the "motiveless malignity" school contends that the question of slavery is irrelevant. Sidney Kaplan, for example, argues that motivation "is not an issue *within the story*."[10] Feltenstein concurs:

"Slavery is not an issue here; the focus is upon evil in action in a certain situation."[11]

Views such as the above make for a relatively simple tale: Babo and his Negro followers are evil; Cereno and the whites are good; Delano is the bewildered observer slow to comprehend the difference between the appearance of good and the reality of evil. This neat parceling out of roles assigns to Melville a racial attitude nowhere evident in his fiction. How unlike the man who emphasized in all his books that men, regardless of color, are essentially alike! Accordingly, Melville's characters in *Benito Cereno* cannot be placed within a strict good-evil framework. White sailors and black slaves, rather than being "whitened" and "blackened," merge into gray, a color which blurs any distinction between them. Interestingly, Melville sets the tone of his tale with an early emphasis on gray:

Everything was mute and calm; everything gray. The sea, though undulated into long roods of swells, seemed fixed, and was sleeked at the surface like waved lead that has cooled and set in the smelter's mould. The sky seemed a gray surtout. Flights of troubled gray foul, kith and kin with flights of troubled gray vapours among which they were mixed, skimmed low and fitfully over the waters, as swallows over meadows before storms. Shadows present, foreshadowing deeper shadows to come.[12]

In the world of gray shadows, this "smelter's pot," humans cannot be readily dichotomized. Man, as evidenced by the duality (i.e., man-devil, lion-lamb) of many of Melville's earlier characters, may evoke both admiration and revulsion. In this connection, Melville offers a revealing observation in his "Sketch Second" of "The Encantadas":

. . . Even the tortoise, dark and melancholy as it is upon the back, still possesses a bright side; its calipee or breast-plate being sometimes of a faint yellowish or golden tinge. Moreover, everyone knows that tortoises as well as turtle are of such a make, that if you but put them on their backs you thereby expose their bright sides without the possibility of their recovering themselves, and turning into view the other. But after you have done this, and because you have done this, you should not swear that the tortoise has no dark side. Enjoy the bright, keep it turned up perpetually if you can, but be honest, and don't deny the black. Neither should he, who cannot turn the tortoise from its natural position so as to hide the darker and expose its livelier aspect, like a great October pumpkin in the sun, for that cause declare the creature to be one total inky blot. The tortoise is both black and bright.[13]

Like the tortoise, Babo and the Negroes aboard the *San Dominick* are neither black (pure evil) nor bright (angels avenging a moral wrong). By showing both sides of whites and blacks, by illustrating the universality of the savage impulse, Melville again dramatizes the sameness of man. But, as Melville says in "The Encantadas," "Let us to particulars."

Trusting and benevolent as Captain Delano is, one cannot ignore the possibility of his being an object of satire, what Charles I. Glicksberg calls "a composite reflection of the righteous stereotyped attitudes prevalent at the time."[14] To the good American captain, "a man of such native simplicity as to be incapable of satire or irony" (p. 90), the Negro is simply not an individual; he takes "humane satisfaction" in seeing the blacks dutifully performing their designated roles in life. He notes the "peculiar love in negroes of uniting industry with pastime" (p. 72), and he is amused by "the African love of bright colours and fine shows" (p. 121). He admires in the Negro servant "that affectionate zeal which transmutes into something filial or fraternal acts in themselves but menial; and which has gained for the negro the repute of making the most pleasing body-servant in the world; one, too, whom a master need be on no stiffly superior terms with, but may treat with familiar trust; less a servant than a devoted companion" (p. 75). To the "blunt thinking" American, the "menial familiarity" of the black servant is marked by the "charm of simple-hearted attachment" (p. 91). That "charm" is also evident in Delano's pastoral view of the female slaves: Negresses are "unsophisticated as leopardesses; loving as doves"; another is "like a doe" and her infant a "wide-awake fawn" (p. 105). In Delano's consciousness no detail of the Negro stereotype is overlooked:

There is something in the negro which, in a peculiar way, fits him for avocations about one's person. Most negroes are natural valets and hair dressers; taking to the comb and brush congenially as to the castanets, and flourishing them apparently with almost equal satisfaction. There is, too, a smooth tact about them in this employment, with a marvellous, noiseless, gliding briskness, not ungraceful in its way, singularly pleasing to behold, and still more so to be the manipulated subject of. And above all is the great gift of good humour. Not the mere grin or laugh is here meant. Those were unsuitable. But a certain easy cheerfulness, harmonious in every glance and gesture; as though God had set the whole negro to some pleasant tune. [P. 120]

The formula continues, adding "the docility arising from the unaspiring contentment of a limited mind and that susceptibility of blind attachment sometimes inhering in indisputable inferiors" (p. 120). Delano's righteous belief in the superiority of the white race is repeatedly emphasized. For example, he dismisses the possibility of collusion between the Spanish and the Negroes by affirming to himself, "Whites . . . by nature, were the shrewder race," and blacks "were too stupid" (p. 108). He also refuses to accept the conventional notion that a mulatto is bound to turn out a devil: it is "not very creditable to us white-skins if a little of our blood mixed with the African's should, far from improving the latter's quality, have the sad effect of pouring vitriolic acid into black broth; improving the hue, perhaps, but not the wholesomeness" (p. 128). The most indicting satirical thrust of all is the revelation that Delano "took to negroes, not philanthropically, but genially, just as other men to Newfoundland dogs" (p. 121). Thus, Captain Amasa Delano of Duxbury, Massachusetts, has "a weakness for negroes" (p. 121). They are excellent and loyal servants, cheerful lovers of color and show, deft handlers of either comb and brush or castanet— in reality, "inferiors" content with their lot as slaves. As a consequence, despite a bizarre and ominous atmosphere on board the *San Dominick,* Delano cannot perceive that the blacks are in rebellion. Even when a Spanish lad is knifed by a Negro boy and a sailor is trampled by two Negroes,

Delano's veil of bias enables him to rationalize. His comfortable assumptions about the Negro character do not allow for the possibility of their being savage; his superficial appraisal does not admit that Negroes might seek their freedom. After all, "Newfoundland dogs" are domesticated and loyal.

Generally, critics have agreed that Delano is self-righteous and naive; some even see in his portrait Melville's indictment of mid-nineteenth-century America. Max Putzel, for example, claims that "Melville seems to question whether this nation's benevolent optimism is more than a form of self-satisfaction based on blindness to the figure we cut with other peoples—especially primitive ones we exploit."[15] Others reflect the same critical bent: Barry Phillips calls Delano a "smug American, priggish, prudent, patronizing";[16] Joseph Schiffman notes that Melville perhaps intended Delano "as a microcosm of American attitudes of the times toward Negroes";[17] Warren D'Azevedo says that "the withering irony created by Captain Delano's patronizing good will might have been too close to satire for the comfort of many northern whites of the mid 1800's."[18] Whether Delano is a representative American or not, his perception is limited. But what does he fail to see? Here the critics diverge. Some argue that his naiveté lies in his failure to see the Negro as an embodiment of evil, others, that he is naive because he cannot see the blacks' desire for freedom. In a sense, both schools are correct; Delano is unable to regard the Negro as a human capable of intelligence and guile, of atrocity and heroism—in short, capable of good and evil.

If Delano's "weakness for Negroes" causes their image to be distorted, what, then, is the reality of the blacks? From the second point of view, the extracts from Cereno's deposition during the trial, we discover that the man whom Delano sees as a solicitous and charming menial is capable of animal savagery. The Negroes murdered "eighteen men of those who were sleeping upon deck, some with handspikes and hatchets, and others by throwing them alive overboard, after tying them" (p. 151). The owner of the slaves, Don Alexandro

Aranda, was dragged mangled and half alive to the deck where his murder was completed before the eyes of Babo. His body, stripped of flesh "in a way which [Benito Cereno], so long as reason is left him, can never divulge" (p. 162), was then mounted below the ship's figurehead to remind the other whites of what could be their fate. The Negresses, had they not been restrained, "would have tortured to death, instead of simply killing, the Spaniards slain by command of the negro Babo" (p. 163). From the deposition we also learn "that the negroes broke an arm of one of the cabin-boys and gave him strokes with hatchets" (p. 163). Another Spaniard had hot tar poured over his hands. Still others, their arms bound, were thrown alive into the sea. Of the thirty-six crewmen, only six remained alive. In this document of horror, Delano's Newfoundland dogs become wolves.

Underscoring the bestiality of the blacks are the animal images frequently attached to them. An elderly Negro "ferreted" into a knotted rope. Family groups of blacks perched in an old longboat are "like a social circle of bats, sheltering in some friendly cave; at intervals ebon flights of naked boys and girls . . . darting in and out of the den's mouth" (p. 117). In the battle between whites and blacks, the Negroes' "red tongues lolled, wolf-like, from their black mouths" (p. 148). His face turned toward Cereno, Babo is "like a shepherd's dog." When Babo's real intentions are known, he is described as "snakishly writhing up" (p. 143) from the bottom of a boat. Elsewhere his head is called a "hive of subtlety." Perhaps the most striking figure of all is the *San Dominick's* stern piece, "medallioned about by groups of mythological or symbolical devices; uppermost and central of which was a dark satyr in a mask, holding his foot on the prostrate neck of a writhing figure, likewise masked" (p. 70). This description, symbolically depicts the true nature of things aboard the slave ship: the "dark satyr," Babo, his true identity masked to Delano, is holding in subjection the "writhing" Cereno, whose identity is also masked. The stern piece is also the key to Babo's nature. He is half man and half beast; as indicated,

Delano sees neither. It is not surprising, then, that many
readers, repelled by the Negro atrocities and by the animal
images, view the blacks as a malignant, destructive force and,
accordingly, empathize with the helpless, victimized whites.
In a sense, such readers have greater perception than Delano;
whereas he acknowledges neither the man nor the beast, they
see at least the beast. The man, however, is also there.

The Negroes in *Benito Cereno* are neither Delano's docile
subservients nor ravenous animals. Both assessments represent an extreme, an indictment of an entire race by a man
whose concern lies with the "common continent of men."
As with the Galapagos tortoise, Melville has not denied the
dark side of the Negroes. But neither are they "one total inky
blot." In this connection, it should be noted that in some
respects the whites are as "dark" as the slaves. The animal
images associated with the slaves likewise characterize the
whites. A mysterious Spanish sailor is "like a fox" (p. 108).
Another's skin is "shrunk up with wrinkles like a pelican's
empty pouch" (p. 109). During one of his suspicious mo-
ments, Delano envisions the velvet of Cereno's dress as "but
the silky paw to his fangs" (p. 93). Called a "somnambulist,"
Cereno is like "a white noddy, a strange fowl, so called from
its lethargic somnambulistic character, being frequently caught
by hand at sea" (p. 69). During the attack on the slaves the
white seamen are described as "submerged sword-fish rush-
ing hither and thither through shoals of black fish" (p. 147).
Spanish boys as well as slave boys are like "pilot-fish within
easy call continually hovering around Don Benito" (p. 76).
Since pilot-fish are the constant companions of sharks, the
logical extension of this analogy attaches to Don Benito the
same viciousness associated with Stubb who to Fleece is
"more of shark dan Massa Shark hisself." It should be noted,
too, that in *Mardi* Melville refers to the shovel-nosed shark
as "lethargic," the same word used to describe Cereno. And
in his poem "The Maldive Shark" Melville's diction in describing the shovel-nosed shark is appropriate for Cereno.
Both are "phlegmatical," "lethargic," and "dull." The simi-

larity of images attached to both blacks and whites can hardly lead to a precise dichotomy of evil and good.

But what happens when the search extends beyond images? How do the whites act when they recapture the *San Dominick*? Do their civilized natures emerge? Are their acts marked by Christian, civilized justice? The deposition provides some answers. In it we find evidence of white barbarity balancing that of the slaves. Several Negroes were killed at night while shackled to the ring bolts on deck. Martinez Gola was caught aiming a razor at the throat of a chained slave. Bartholomew Barlo was stopped from stabbing a shackled black. Perhaps the most damning illustration of white barbarity is the account of Babo's punishment: "dragged to the gibbet at the tail of a mule, the black met his voiceless end. The body was burned to ashes; but for many days the head, that hive of subtlety, fixed on a pole in the Plaza,' met, unabashed, the gaze of the whites" (p. 170). Allen Guttman sees this final paragraph as "the triumph of Babo's sheer and literally disembodied will."[19] It seems more accurate to view the description of Babo's execution as an indictment of a society which, even within the framework of law, is as capable of barbarity as is the "unenlightened" savage. Significantly, Melville left a record of his reaction to executions such as Babo's; in *Typee* he raises an uncomfortable question:

I ask whether the mere eating of human flesh so very far exceeds in barbarity that custom which only a few years since was practised in enlightened England:—a convicted traitor, perhaps a man found guilty of honesty, patriotism, and such like heinous crimes, had his head lopped off with a huge axe, his bowels dragged out and thrown into a fire; while his body, carved into four quarters, was with his head exposed upon pikes, and permitted to rot and fester among the public haunts of men![20]

Nine years after *Typee*, Babo's death is strikingly similar to that described here. To recast Melville's question—does the barbarity of the black slaves exceed that of a white Christian court? By reserving Babo's death for the final paragraph and thereby emphasizing it, Melville reinforces what, throughout his fiction, he repeatedly stated—that no great disparity exists between the nonwhite savage and the white civilized man. The severed black head facing St. Bartholomew's church— an ironic and tragic juxtaposition of two worlds, two cultures, two races—renders incredible the argument that Melville has "whitened the whites." Following the above passage from *Typee,* Melville indicted "the white as the most ferocious animal on the face of the earth." In *Benito Cereno,* he shows both white and black as equally capable of ferocity, equally capable of reducing men to the level of brutes. Babo, it should be noted, was a slave in both black and white societies. In merging the "civilized" brutality of the whites with the animal ferocity of the blacks, Melville has dramatized the universality of the savage impulse.

If the whites have their "dark" side, the slaves have their "bright." The Negroes as a group, for example, are a compact, well-disciplined unit: "All the negroes, though not in the first place knowing to the design of revolt, when it was accomplished, approved it" (p. 161). While defending the *San Dominick* against the white counterattack, the slaves fought united, "scorning peace or truce" (p. 148). That every Negro on board, "down to the youngest negress," was a carefully drilled and obedient recruit in the plot to deceive Delano is, as Delano himself conjectures, "an incredible inference" (p. 99). It is also a compliment to their resolve and to their capacity for self-rule. Also on the bright side is the striking portrait of the revolt's co-leader Atufal who, according to the deposition, "committed no murder." Delano admires his "colossal form" and sees "royal spirit" in him. He was a king in his own land, and his bearing is evidence of his title. A "gigantic black," he stands in unquailing muteness before the pathetic figure of Cereno. Atufal reminds one of the superb Daggoo; Cereno standing face to face with this king recalls Melville's observation in *Moby-Dick* that a "white man standing before him [Daggoo] seemed a white flag come to beg truce of a fortress."

Even Babo deserves some defense. He is not a black Iago, not the exemplar of natural human depravity which some critics brand him. In the first place, he has a motive—freedom from the white man's bondage and desire to return home. The deposition makes clear that Babo's principal objective is to be carried to Senegal or to the neighboring islands of St. Nicholas and that the Negroes "would do and conform themselves to everything the deponent [Benito Cereno] should require as to eating and drinking" (p. 152) in order to facilitate the journey home. We learn, too, that Babo and Atufal "held daily conferences, in which they discussed what was necessary for their design of returning to Senegal" (p. 153). Even the murder of Alexandro was ordered because Babo and his followers "could not otherwise be sure of their liberty" (p. 154), and the skeleton figurehead was a warning to "keep faith with the blacks from here to Senegal" (p. 156). Babo's quest for home is also evident in his sparing the life of Raneds, a "good navigator." Finally, when Babo tries to stab Cereno, his one attempt to murder, his face is "lividly vindictive" (p. 143). The slavery issue may not be central to *Benito Cereno,* but to call Babo motiveless is to ignore the evidence. His cruel tyranny was dictated by his desire for freedom and implicitly by his sense of manhood. To be a thrall, *Mardi* reminds us, is to be "unmanned." In several respects Babo's revolt is a dramatic realization of the freedom-slavery discussions in *Mardi.* Intriguing links between the two works are difficult to ignore. Yoomy would have hailed the uprising: "All honest hearts must cheer this tribe of Hamo on; though they cut their chains with blades thrice edged, and gory to the haft! 'Tis right to fight for freedom, whoever be the thrall." Media accurately predicts the response of the whites: "Were these serfs to rise . . . like dogs, they would be hunted down." Babbalanja angrily stamps slavery "a blot, foul as the crater-pool of hell." And we cannot help recalling Yoomy's prophecy: "No misery born of crime, but spreads and poisons wide."[21]

Babo also deserves considerable credit for being the awesomely clever mastermind of a plot so well implemented that it almost succeeds. The intricacy of his plan is evident in the following extract:

. . . The negro Babo then announced the plan to all his companions, which pleased them; that he then, the better to disguise
the truth, devised many expedients, in some of them uniting deceit
and defence; that of this sort was the device of the six Ashantees
before-named, who were his braves; that them he stationed on the
break of the poop, as if to clean certain hatchets . . . but in reality
to use them, and distribute them at need, and at a given word he
told them; that, among other devices, was the device of presenting
Atufal . . . as chained, though in a moment the chains could be
dropped; that in every particular he informed the deponent what
part he was expected to enact in every device, and what story he
was to tell on every occasion . . . ; that, conscious that many of
the negroes would be turbulent, the negro Babo appointed the
four aged negroes . . . to keep what domestic order they could
on the decks; that again and again he harangued the Spaniards
and his companions, informing them of his intent, and of his devices, and of the invented story that the deponent was to tell; . . .
that these arrangements were made and matured during the in-
terval of two or three hours, between their first sighting the ship
and the arrival on board of Captain Amasa Delano. [Pp. 158–59]

The mind that devised such a scheme may be a "hive of
subtlety," but it is a mind which commands respect. Central
to that scheme is Babo's masquerade as a menial. Like the
mask of the confidence man, it is based on a shrewd understanding of the white man's attitudes toward the black. Babo
is also to be respected for his determination and spirit. Never
panicking, never faltering, even during the fury of the revolt,
he steadfastly keeps in mind the main objective. Neither does
he bow; captured, "he uttered no sound, and could not be
forced to" (p. 169). And like the unquailing, kingly Atufal
before the sickly Cereno, Babo even in death remains defiant,
his head meeting "unabashed, the gaze of the whites." De-
pending on the degree to which one can sympathize with
Babo's motives, the black's performance could be called
heroic. One thing is certain: Babo is no inferior. His dominant
traits are intelligence, determination, firmness of will and command, and defiant pride. Except in the beclouded mind of Delano, the stereotype darky complete with castanets and good-
natured grin is not aboard the *San Dominick;* an individual
is. We may admire or despise Babo, but our response is not

dictated by his color; Melville has created a memorable human being.

We cannot leave *Benito Cereno* without noting Melville's marvelous handling of the slave ship itself. Robin Magowan has noted that "in the *San Dominick* there is portrayed a world mortally corroded by the use to which it has been put, a sham world in which decay has taken on the allure of life."[22] "Mortally corroded" it is, for almost every detail surrounding the vessel suggests death, an appropriate atmosphere for the ship which seamen of the time called a "floating coffin." The *San Dominick* seems launched "from Ezekiel's Valley of Dry Bones." The forecastle, "battered and mouldy," seems "some ancient turret . . . left to decay." Sea-grass "like mourning weeds . . . slimily" smears the ship's name with every "hearse-like roll of the hull." The sound of the ship's bell is a "dreary graveyard toll." The dead-lights are "all closed like coppered eyes of the coffined," and the state-cabin door is "caulked fast like a sarcophagus lid." The *San Dominick* is indeed a "floating coffin"—an apt setting for the destructive impulses of men both white and black.

Benito Cereno is neither an abolitionist tract nor a condemnation of the Negro race. Evil and ferocity are not confined to the blacks; heroism and virtue are not the exclusive traits of the whites. Both blacks and whites are part of the humanity whose dark side Melville will not deny. Like the satyr on the stern-piece, Babo is part man, part beast. Like Bembo of *Omoo,* he is man (in that his response to humiliation is courageously human) and devil (in that his vengeance takes a particularly vicious turn) But the white man, who ironically espouses a religion of charity, forgiveness, and brotherhood, is also a beast. Who can say where the blame rests for the carnage unleashed aboard the floating coffin?[23] The untamed and demoniac forces rampant on the *San Dominick* characterize not a particular race, but all of mankind. *Benito Cereno* poses the problem with which Herman Melville grappled from *Typee* to *Billy Budd:* the "primeval savageness which ever slumbers in human kind, civilized or uncivilized."

10. "THE COMMON CONTINENT OF MEN"

> *In Liverpool, now half a century ago, I saw*
> *under the shadow of the great dingy street-*
> *wall of Prince's Dock . . . a common sailor, so*
> *intensely black that he must needs have been*
> *a native African of the unadulterate blood of*
> *Ham. A symmetric figure much above the*
> *average height. The two ends of a gay silk*
> *handkerchief thrown loose about the neck*
> *danced upon the displayed ebony of his chest;*
> *in his ears were big hoops of gold, and a*
> *Scotch Highland bonnet with tartan band set*
> *off his shapely head.*
>
> *It was a hot noon in July; and his face,*
> *lustrous with perspiration, beamed with bar-*
> *baric good-humour. In jovial sallies right and*
> *left, his white teeth flashing into view, he*
> *rollicked along, the centre of a company of*
> *his shipmates. These were made up of such an*
> *assortment of tribes and complexions as would*
> *have well fitted them to be marched up by*
> *Anacharsis Cloots before the bar of the first*
> *French Assembly as Representatives of the*
> *Human Race.*
>
> —Herman Melville, *Billy Budd*

A belief in human equality based on "that immaculate manliness we feel within ourselves, so far within us, that it remains

intact though all the outer character seem gone"[1] is central to Melville's racial attitudes. From *Typee* through *Billy Budd* white men and dark, civilized and uncivilized, Christian and heathen, master and servant merge into an Anacharsis Clootz deputation—a "piebald parliament" wherein the man, not the skin color, has importance.

In Melville's fiction the several races of mankind are inseparably intertwined, united by his acknowledgment of the individual's special worth. Through the interaction of characters of all colors, Melville dramatizes how in the ideal society the nonwhite should be regarded. The foolish, the cruel, the ignorant, and the sheltered categorize the nonwhite in accord with the role the "bland hypocrisies" of society assign him, that of inferior buffoon or of scowling savage; the humane and the wise see him as an individual to be liked or disliked for his human traits. This study has shown Melville to be one of the humane and wise. In his fictional world, men have a fundamental claim to humanity. Such democratic faith is echoed and reechoed from the first book to the last. We see that faith in Tommo's warm admiration of the physical perfection and the harmonious social order of the "savage" Polynesians; in his indictment of the white race, which, in imposing its values on the Polynesians, is responsible for corroding the racial identity of these people; in the anger and pity evoked by the plight of Negro slaves in *Mardi;* in Redburn's recognition of the black man's humanity; in White-Jacket's acknowledgment of man, white or dark, as the image of God; in the "champions from the kingly commons," dark as well as white, embraced by Ishmael's "just spirit of equality"; in the striking resemblances between General Glendinning, John Paul Jones and Ethan Allen, and the Typee warriors and Queequeg; in the universe of *The Confidence-Man* and *Benito Cereno,* where black is indistinguishable from white; and, finally, in the simple recognition that the "handsome sailor"—a cynosure of "strength and beauty"—can be either a Billy Budd or a Negro on a Liverpool dock.

The barrier to equality, Melville suggests, is the absence of mutual respect which, in turn, becomes mutual distrust. Significantly, the white man is usually the architect of the wall which separates the races. If Melville's nonwhites are scowling barbarians or grinning stereotypes, they are made so by the whites who refuse to acknowledge their humanity. The denial takes many forms: "wanton acts of cruelty" for "mere amusement" by white seamen who "hardly consider [Polynesians] human"; the humiliation and endless rounds of practical jokes inflicted on black seacooks; the brute level to which Negro slaves are degraded by the lash; the stares and grimaces of local greenhorns at the Queequegs, Samoas, and Lavenders; a Spaniard's racial insult flung at Daggoo; Stubb's abandoning "insignificant" Pip and ridiculing Fleece; river-boat passengers tossing pennies at the mouth of a crippled Negro; an American captain's fondness for Negroes as though they were Newfoundland dogs.

Such treatment is best explained by White-Jacket: ". . . There is something in us, somehow, that in the most degraded condition, we snatch at a chance to deceive ourselves into a fancied superiority to others, whom we suppose lower in the scale than ourselves."[2] Melville's fictional world refutes this self-deception, this "fancied superiority" which degrades others. There can be no preeminent race, no mastery of one people over another in a world where white American heroes are remarkably similar to dusky Polynesians; where "the New Zealander's tattooing is not a prodigy nor the Chinaman's way an enigma"; where "we may have civilized bodies and yet barbarous souls"; where "primeval savageness ever slumbers in human kind, civilized or uncivilized"; where "a man can be honest in any sort of skin"; where Indians, Orientals, Polynesians, Negroes, and Caucasians are "sprung from one head, and made in one image." Such a world, dark as well as bright, is Herman Melville's "common continent of men."

NOTES

INTRODUCTION

1. Merrell R. Davis and William H. Gilman, eds., *The Letters of Herman Melville* (New Haven: Yale University Press, 1960), p. 92.

2. Herman Melville, *Moby-Dick, The Works of Herman Melville,* VII–VIII (1922; rpt. New York: Russell and Russell, 1963), VII, 144. Subsequent references to *Moby-Dick* are to this edition (R. & R. rpt.) and are made parenthetically in the text.

3. *Herman Melville: The Tragedy of Mind* (1944; rpt. New York: Russell and Russell, 1962), p. 94.

4. *The Power of Blackness* (New York: Vintage Books, 1958), p. 190.

5. Introduction, *Herman Melville: Representative Selections* (New York: American Book Company, 1938), p. xcvii.

6. *The Fine Hammered Steel of Herman Melville* (Urbana: University of Illinois Press, 1957), p. 108.

7. *The Wake of the Gods: Melville's Mythology* (Stanford: Stanford University Press, 1963), p. 145.

8. Ibid., p. 150.

9. Introduction, *Short Novels of the Masters* (New York: Rinehart, 1962), p. 10.

10. *Herman Melville* (New York: William Sloane, 1950), p. 240.

11. "Melville's *Benito Cereno,*" *American Literature,* 19 (November, 1947), 247.

12. See, for example, F. O. Matthiessen, *American Renaissance* (New York: Oxford University Press, 1941), p. 508; James E. Miller, Jr., *A Reader's Guide to Herman Melville* (New York:

The Noonday Press, 1962), p. 159; and *The Power of Blackness,*
p. 190. For an excellent collection of *Benito Cereno* criticism, see
Seymour L. Gross, ed., *A Benito Cereno Handbook* (Belmont:
Wadsworth Publishing Company, 1965).
13. *Letters of Herman Melville,* p. 130.
14. Herman Melville, *Israel Potter, The Works of Herman Melville* (R. & R. rpt.), XI, 81–82.
15. I have violated chronology once—by treating *Benito Cereno*
last. The subject matter is an appropriate climax to my focus.

1. TYPEE

1. Introduction, *The Portable Melville* (New York: The Viking
Press, 1952), p. xi.
2. Introduction, *The Shorter Novels of Herman Melville* (New
York: Fawcett Publications, 1964), p. 30.
3. *Fine Hammered Steel,* p. 65.
4. *Typee: A Peep at Polynesian Life,* ed. Harrison Hayford,
Hershel Parker, and G. Thomas Tanselle, *The Writings of Herman
Melville* (Evanston, Ill.: Northwestern University Press), I,
(1968), 5. Subsequent references to *Typee* are to this edition
(N.-N. ed.) and are made parenthetically in the text.
5. *Power of Blackness,* p. 173.
6. *Billy Budd and Other Prose Pieces,* ed. Raymond W. Weaver,
The Works of Herman Melville (R. & R. rpt.), XIII, 11.
7. Ibid., 15.
8. *Herman Melville: The Tragedy of Mind,* p. 26.
9. Ibid., p. 27.
10. *Fine Hammered Steel,* p. 52.
11. *Melville in the South Seas* (New York: Dover Publications,
1966), p. 302.
12. *Herman Melville,* p. 57.
13. *Herman Melville: A Study of His Life and Vision* (New
York: Harcourt, Brace and World, 1962), p. 43.
14. *Herman Melville: The Tragedy of Mind,* p. 20.
15. *Herman Melville: A Biography* (Berkeley: University of
California Press, 1951), p. 53.
16. *Melville in the South Seas,* p. 193.
17. In *Typee* Melville twice comments sympathetically on the
American Indian. In addition to the above, he observes in a later
chapter: "The hospitality of the wild Arab, the courage of the
North American Indian, and the faithful friendships of some of
the Polynesian nations, far surpass anything of a similar kind
among the polished communities of Europe" (pp. 202–03).
18. *Reader's Guide to Herman Melville,* pp. 33–34.

2. OMOO

1. *Melville in the South Seas,* p. 197.
2. *Omoo: A Narrative of Adventures in the South Seas, The*

Writings of Herman Melville (N.-N. ed.), II (1968), 6–7. Subsequent references to *Omoo* are to this edition and are made parenthetically in the text.
3. *Herman Melville,* p. 70.
4. *Herman Melville: A Biography,* p. 60.
5. Milton R. Stern, *The Fine Hammered Steel,* p. 64.
6. For the account of the fight according to official records, see Leon Howard, *Herman Melville: A Biography,* p. 57. According to Howard, James Watts (Sidney Ben) responded to Benbow's (Bembo's) orders "with certain anatomical suggestions."

3. MARDI

1. *Mardi and A Voyage Thither, The Writings of Herman Melville* (N.-N. ed), III (1970), xvii. Subsequent references to *Mardi* are to this edition and are made parenthetically in the text.
2. Howard P. Vincent, *The Trying-Out of Moby-Dick* (Carbondale: Southern Illinois University Press, 1949), p. 27.
3. *Pacifism and Rebellion in the Writings of Herman Melville* (The Hague: Mouton, 1964), p. 32.
4. *The Example of Melville* (Princeton: Princeton University Press, 1962), p. 28.
5. The "Newfoundland dog" figure recurs in Melville's fiction. For example, Guinea of *The Confidence-Man,* Babo of *Benito Cereno,* and Queequeg of *Moby-Dick* are all compared to this domestic creature, in the first two cases to suggest subservience, and in the last to suggest docility and good nature. As for Samoa, it must be admitted that the comparison hints more at his comic side than at his savagery.
6. Cholos are half-breed Spaniards who, the narrator notes, are "notorious for their unscrupulous villainy" (p. 69). Yet one of Melville's most moving characters is the Chola Widow of "Sketch Eighth" in "The Encantadas." Her story is a testimony to a human's courageous struggle for life: "She seemed as one who, having experienced the sharpest of mortal pangs, was henceforth content to have all lesser heartstrings riven, one by one. To Hunilla, pain seemed so necessary, that pain in other beings, though by love and sympathy made her own, was unrepiningly to be borne. A heart of yearning in a frame of steel. A heart of earthly yearning, frozen by the frost which falleth from the sky." (*The Piazza Tales, The Works of Herman Melville* (R. & R. rpt.), X, 235). Her tale evokes from Melville this tribute: "Humanity, thou strong thing, I worship thee, not in the laurelled victor, but in this vanquished one" (p. 227).
7. Introduction, *Mardi* (New York: Capricorn Books, 1964), p. vi.
8. In some measure, Samoa is a forerunner of Queequeg in *Moby-Dick.* Both are ugly figures who in their physical prowess command respect and awe; both are self-possessed and practical.

9. *Pacifism and Rebellion,* p. 35.
10. *Fine Hammered Steel,* p. 125.
11. Introduction, *Mardi,* p. vi.
12. *Reader's Guide to Herman Melville,* p. 51.
13. *American Renaissance* (New York: Oxford University Press, 1941), p. 384.
14. *Fine Hammered Steel,* p. 125.
15. *American Renaissance,* p. 383.
16. Introduction, *Herman Melville: Representative Selections,* p. cx.
17. Ronald Mason in *The Spirit above the Dust* (London: John Lehmann, 1951), p. 56, also argues for Babbalanja's being Melville's spokesman: ". . . Melville's acute intelligence, his broad and sensitive humanism, are revealed in this figure [Babbalanja] as in no other of his full-length characters in all his literary career."
18. Hennig Cohen, ed. (New York: Thomas Yoseloff, 1964), p. 197.
19. *Herman Melville* (London: Macmillan, 1926), p. 105.
20. *The Battle-Pieces of Herman Melville* (New York: Thomas Yoseloff, 1964), p. 197.

4. REDBURN

1. *Redburn: His First Voyage, The Writings of Herman Melville* (N.-N. ed.), IV (1969), 5. Subsequent references to *Redburn* are to this edition and are indicated parenthetically in the text.
2. *Pacifism and Rebellion,* p. 57.
3. *White-Jacket, or The World in a Man-of-War, The Writings of Herman Melville* (N.-N. ed.), V (1970), 32.
4. Ibid., 10.
5. Ibid.
6. *Spirit above the Dust,* p. 76.
7. *Herman Melville: The Tragedy of Mind,* p. 66.

5. WHITE-JACKET

1. *White-Jacket, or The World in a Man-of-War,* The Writings of Herman Melville (N.-N. ed), V (1970), 398. Subsequent references to *White-Jacket* are to this edition and are made parenthetically in the text.
2. *Spirit above the Dust,* p. 81.
3. Introduction, *White-Jacket* by Herman Melville (New York: Holt, Rinehart and Winston, 1967), p. xx.
4. Ibid., p. xxxvi.
5. *Herman Melville: A Biography,* p. 72.
6. Quoted by Seymour L. Gross in "Introduction: Stereotype to Archetype: The Negro in American Literary Criticism," in *Images of the Negro in American Literature,* ed. Seymour L. Gross and

John Edward Hardy (Chicago: University of Chicago Press, 1966), p. 7.
7. *Melville in the South Seas*, p. 433. Anderson notes that the presiding judge was Melville's future father-in-law Chief Justice Lemuel Shaw, and that he testified to the slaveowner's admirable and humane conduct.
8. Mark Winsome in Melville's *The Confidence-Man* is such a person; a mystical philosopher shielded by his remoteness from human considerations, he is the object of Melville's satirical barbs.
9. *Works of Herman Melville* (R. & R. rpt.), xii, 149.

6. MOBY-DICK

1. "Mr. Parkman's Tour," *Literary World*, 113 (March 31, 1849), 291.
2. Ibid.
3. Herman Melville, *Moby-Dick*. See note 2 in introduction for complete bibliographical data.
4. Anacharsis Clootz (1755–94) appeared before the French National Assembly in 1790, leading a gathering of foreigners, thus dramatizing the sympathy of all mankind with the French Revolution.
5. *Power of Blackness*, p. 177.
6. *Trying-Out of Moby-Dick*, p. 105.
7. *Reader's Guide to Herman Melville*, p. 93.
8. *Love and Death in the American Novel* (1960; rpt. Cleveland: Meridian, 1962), p. 530.
9. *Spirit above the Dust*, pp. 143–44.
10. *Trying-Out of Moby-Dick*, p. 105.
11. *Herman Melville: The Tragedy of Mind*, p. 13.
12. *Trying-Out of Moby-Dick*, p. 78.
13. Despite my indebtedness to Howard P. Vincent, it should be noted that Vincent errs in saying that Queequeg was "shanghaied by whalemen and carried against his will to the shores of New England" (*Trying-Out of Moby-Dick*, p. 76). The text unmistakably indicates that Queequeg acted of his own volition:

A Sag Harbour ship visited his father's bay, and Queequeg sought a passage to Christian lands. But the ship, having her full complement of seamen, spurned his suit; and not all the King his father's influence could prevail. But Queequeg vowed a vow. Alone in his canoe, he paddled off to a distant strait, which he knew the ship must pass through when she quitted the island. . . . When the ship was gliding by, like a flash he darted out; gained her side; with one backward dash of his foot capsized and sank his canoe; climbed up the chains; and throwing himself at full length upon the deck, grappled a ring-bolt there, and swore not to let it go, though hacked to pieces.

In vain the captain threatened to throw him overboard; suspended a cutlass over his naked wrists; Queequeg was the son of a King, and Queequeg budged not. Struck by his desperate dauntlessness, and his wild desire to visit Christendom, the captain at last relented, and told him he might make himself at home. [VII, 68–69]

14. *Reader's Guide to Herman Melville,* p. 113.
15. During the composition of *Moby-Dick,* Melville wrote in a letter to Hawthorne, "I read Solomon more and more, and every time see deeper and deeper and unspeakable meanings in him." *Letters of Herman Melville,* p. 130. In *Moby-Dick* Ishmael also refers to Solomon: ". . . that mortal man who hath more of joy than sorrow in him . . . cannot be true—not true, or undeveloped. With books the same. The truest of all men was the Man of Sorrows, and the truest of all books is Solomon's, and Ecclesiastes is the fine hammered steel of woe. 'All is vanity.' ALL. This wilful world hath not got hold of unchristian Solomon's wisdom yet" (VIII, 181–82).
16. To a dissension-ridden, post-Civil War America, Melville offers the same remedy: "Let us be Christians toward our fellow-whites, as well as philanthropists toward the blacks, our fellow-men. In all things and toward all, we are enjoined to do as we would be done by." *Battle-Pieces of Herman Melville,* p. 200.
17. *Trying-Out of Moby-Dick,* p. 77.
18. *Reader's Guide to Herman Melville,* p. 114.
19. Paralleling this ironic contradiction is Ishmael's reaction to the whiteness of Moby-Dick. White, traditionally the color associated with beauty, virtue, and goodness, strikes terror into Ishmael's heart. Conversely, the darkness of Queequeg is associated with good. Likewise, black Pip, the cabin boy, is given "heavenly" wisdom and has a good heart.
20. This association of darkness and manly strength recalls the Tahitian saying in *Omoo,* "If dark the cheek of the mother, / The son will sound the war conch" (p. 129).
21. "Melville's 'Isolatoes',￼" *PMLA,* 60 (December 1945), 1145.
22. *American Renaissance,* p. 416.
23. *Spirit above the Dust,* p. 143.
24. *Love and Death in the American Novel,* p. 541.
25. *Herman Melville,* p. 192.
26. "In Nomine Diaboli," *NEQ,* 24 (December 1951), 443.
27. *American Renaissance,* p. 432.
28. *Herman Melville: A Critical Study,* p. 84.
29. *The Example of Melville,* p. 106.
30. *The Trying-Out of Moby-Dick,* p. 233.
31. Ibid., p. 234.
32. *Billy Budd and Other Prose Pieces,* ed. Raymond W. Weaver, *The Works of Herman Melville* (R. & R. rpt.), XIII, 268–69.

33. "Holiness" here undoubtedly refers to the heavenly wisdom acquired by Pip, but it could also emphasize Melville's repeated reference to man as an image of the creator.

34. *Herman Melville* (New York, 1963), p. 104.

7. *PIERRE* AND *ISRAEL POTTER*

1. *Letters of Herman Melville,* p. 146.

2. Ibid.

3. When applied to the entire novel, this description could well be ironic; as Howard points out, however, "It seems reasonably clear . . . that Melville did not intend to write the 'impure' book which his critics denounced." *Herman Melville: A Biography,* p. 194.

4. *Letters of Herman Melville,* p. 150.

5. *Pierre, or the Ambiguities, The Writings of Herman Melville* (N.-N. ed), VII (1971), 30. Subsequent references to *Pierre* are to this edition and are made parenthetically in the text.

6. Published first in nine installments, July, 1854, through March, 1855, by *Putnam's Monthly Magazine.*

7. *Letters of Herman Melville,* p. 170.

8. *Israel Potter, The Works of Herman Melville* (R. & R. rpt.), XI, 131. Subsequent references to *Israel Potter* are to this edition and are made parenthetically in the text.

8. *THE CONFIDENCE-MAN*

1. *The Confidence-Man, The Works of Herman Melville* (R. & R. rpt.), XII, 9. Subsequent references to *The Confidence-Man* are to this edition and are made parenthetically in the text.

2. *Mardi, The Writings of Herman Melville* (N-N. ed.), III, 603.

3. *Herman Melville: A Critical Study,* p. 205.

4. *Herman Melville,* pp. 250–51.

5. *Herman Melville: A Study of His Life and Vision,* p. 175.

6. *Melville's Religious Thought: An Essay in Interpretation* (New York: Pageant Books, 1959), p. 115.

7. *Herman Melville: A Biography,* p. 232.

8. *Wake of the Gods,* p. 154.

9. Representative are Franklin, who notes that "the savior is most probably the destroyer" (*Wake of the Gods,* p. 155); Thompson, who says, "Melville liked to play with the concept that the Devil is one of God's most efficient agents in gathering valuable evidence and in carrying out God's own malicious purposes" (*Melville's Quarrel with God,* p. 305); Chase, who sees him as "a cruel, chimerical mask of Christ" (*Herman Melville,* pp. 187–88); and Daniel G. Hoffman, who calls him "a mock-Christ, devilishly quoting Scripture to his purpose" ("The Confidence-Man: His Masquerade," from *Form and Fable in American Fiction,* p. 295).

10. "Sources and Symbols for Melville's *Confidence-Man*" *PMLA*, 66 (June, 1951), 368.

11. *"The Confidence-Man*: His Guises," *PMLA*, 74 (March, 1959), 105.

12. *Israel Potter, The Works of Herman Melville* (R. & R. rpt.), XI, 124.

13. Introduction, *The Confidence-Man* (New York: Holt, Rinehart and Winston, 1964), p. xi.

14. *Herman Melville: A Critical Study*, p. 186.

15. Another white man aboard the *Fidele*, a cynical Missourian, also sees the Negro as a formula. His attitude toward slaves is the exclamation: ". . . Won't have 'em! Bad enough to see whites ducking and grinning round for a favor, without having those poor devils of niggers congeeing round for their corn" (pp. 148–49).

16. *Wake of the Gods*, p. 187.

17. "Melville's Ship of Fools," *PMLA*, 75 (December, 1960), 606.

18. *American Renaissance*, p. 410.

19. The source of the account of the Indian-hater is James Hall's *Sketches of History, Life, and Manners, in the West* (1835).

20. Introduction, *The Confidence-Man*, p. xvi.

21. "Sources and Symbols for Melville's *Confidence-Man*," 376.

22. Ibid., 377.

23. Ibid., 379.

24. "Melville's Indian-Hater: A Note on a Meaning of *The Confidence-Man*," *PMLA*, 67 (December, 1952), 942–43.

25. In this respect, perhaps Moredock's tale is not so much a parable of racial hatred as it is a parable of the misanthrope. The Indians, it should be noted, seem more representative of mankind than of a particular race.

26. "Melville's Indian-Hater," 942.

27. *"The Confidence-Man*: His Masquerade," p. 303.

28. "Melville's Indian-Hater," 948.

29. No. 113, p. 291.

30. *Herman Melville: The Tragedy of Mind*, p. 192.

9. BENITO CERENO

1. Introduction, *Short Novels of the Masters*, p. 10.

2. *Herman Melville*, p. 233.

3. Ibid., p. 240.

4. *Wake of the Gods*, p. 145.

5. Ibid., p. 15.

6. *Herman Melville: A Biography*, p. 219.

7. Ibid., p. 220.

8. Melville's *Benito Cereno*," 247.

9. *American Renaissance*, p. 508.

10. "Herman Melville and the American National Sin," *Journal of Negro History,* 41 (January, 1957), 20.

11. "Melville's *Benito Cereno,*" 255.

12. *The Piazza Tales, The Works of Herman Melville* (R. & R. rpt.), x, 66. Subsequent references to *Benito Cereno* are to this edition and are made parenthetically in the text.

13. Ibid., pp. 188–89.

14. "Melville and the Negro Problem," *Phylon,* 11 (autumn, 1950), 209.

15. "The Sources and the Symbols of Melville's *Benito Cereno,*" *American Literature,* 34 (May, 1962), 196.

16. " 'The Good Captain': A Reading of *Benito Cereno,*" *Texas Studies in Literature and Language,* 4 (summer, 1962), 191.

17. "Critical Problems in Melville's *Benito Cereno,*" *Modern Language Quarterly,* 11 (September, 1950), 322.

18. "Revolt on the *San Dominick,*" *Phylon,* 17 (June, 1956), 140.

19. "The Enduring Innocence of Captain Amasa Delano," *Boston University Studies in English,* 5 (spring, 1961), 44.

20. *The Writings of Herman Melville* (N.-N. ed), I, 125.

21. Ibid., III, 534–35.

22. "Masque and Symbol in Melville's *Benito Cereno,*" *College English,* 23 (February, 1962), 348.

23. Apprehensive about racial strife in the aftermath of the Civil War, Melville could indict neither black man nor white: "Especially in the present transition period for both races in the South, more or less of trouble may not unreasonably be anticipated; but let us not hereafter be too swift to charge the blame exclusively in any one quarter. With certain evils men must be more or less patient." *Battle-Pieces of Herman Melville,* p. 200.

LIST OF WORKS CITED

1. Herman Melville, *Moby-Dick, The Works of Herman Melville* (R. & R. rpt.), VII, 143–44.
2. *The Writings of Herman Melville* (N.-N. ed.), V, 277.

LIST OF WORKS CITED

Anderson, Charles Roberts. *Melville in the South Seas.* New York: Dover Publications, 1966.

Arvin, Newton. *Herman Melville.* New York: William Sloane, 1950.

Bernstein, John. *Pacifism and Rebellion in the Writings of Herman Melville.* The Hague: Mouton, 1964.

Berthoff, Warner. *The Example of Melville.* Princeton: Princeton University Press, 1962.

Braswell, William. *Melville's Religious Thought: An Essay in Interpretation.* New York: Pageant Books, 1959.

Chase, Richard. *Herman Melville: A Critical Study.* New York: Macmillan, 1949.

Cohen, Hennig, ed. *The Battle-Pieces of Herman Melville.* New York: Thomas Yoseloff, 1964.

———. Introduction to *The Confidence-Man* by Herman Melville. New York: Holt, Rinehart and Winston, 1964.

———. Introduction to *White-Jacket* by Herman Melville. New York: Holt, Rinehart and Winston, 1967.

Davis, Merrill R. and William H. Gilman, eds. *The Letters of Herman Melville.* New Haven: Yale University Press, 1960.

D'Azevedo, Warren. "Revolt on the *San Dominick.*" *Phylon,* 17 (June, 1956), 129–40.

Feltenstein, Rosalie. "Melville's *Benito Cereno.*" *American Literature,* 19 (November, 1947), 245–55.

Fiedler, Leslie. *Love and Death in the American Novel.* New York: Criterion, 1960; rpt. Cleveland: Meridian, 1962.

Franklin, H. Bruce. *The Wake of the Gods: Melville's Mythology.* Stanford: Stanford University Press, 1963.

————. Introduction to *Mardi* by Herman Melville. New York: Capricorn, 1964.

Freeman, John. *Herman Melville.* London: Macmillan, 1926.

Glicksberg, Charles I. "Melville and the Negro Problem." *Phylon,* 11 (autumn, 1950), 207–15.

Gross, Seymour L. and John Edward Hardy, eds. *Images of the Negro in American Literature.* Chicago: University of Chicago Press, 1966.

Guttman, Allen. "The Enduring Innocence of Captain Amasa Delano." *Boston University Studies in English,* 5 (spring, 1961), 35–45.

Hillway, Tyrus. *Herman Melville.* New York: Twayne, 1963.

Hoffman, Daniel G. *"The Confidence-Man:* His Masquerade," from *Form and Fable in American Fiction.* New York: Oxford University Press, 1961.

Howard, Leon. *Herman Melville: A Biography.* Berkeley: University of California Press, 1951.

Kaplan, Sidney. "Herman Melville and the American National Sin." *Journal of Negro History,* 41 (October, 1956), 311–38, 42 (January, 1957), 11–37.

————. "Herman Melville and the American National Sin." Doctoral dissertation, Harvard University, 1959.

Levin, Harry. *The Power of Blackness: Hawthorne, Poe, Melville.* New York: Vintage Books, 1958.

Leyda, Jay, ed. Introduction to *The Portable Melville.* New York: The Viking Press, 1952.

Magowan, Robin. "Masque and Symbol in Melville's *Benito Cereno.*" *College English,* 23 (February, 1962), 346–51.

Mason, Ronald. *The Spirit above the Dust: A Study of Herman Melville.* London: John Lehmann, 1951.

Matthiessen, F. O. *American Renaissance.* New York: Oxford University Press, 1941.

Melville, Herman. "Mr. Parkman's Tour." *The Literary World,* 113 (March 31, 1849), 291–93.

————. *The Works of Herman Melville,* 16 vols. London: Constable, 1922–24; rpt. New York: Russell and Russell, 1963.

————. *The Writings of Herman Melville: The Northwestern-Newberry Edition,* gen. ed. Harrison Hayford. Vols. I–V, VII. Evanston and Chicago: Northwestern University Press and the Newberry Library, 1968–71. This edition, which will be standard, is currently in progress.

Miller, James E., Jr. *A Reader's Guide to Herman Melville.* New York: The Noonday Press, 1962.

Miller, James E., Jr. "*The Confidence-Man:* His Guises." *PMLA,* 74 (March, 1959), 102–11.

Mumford, Lewis. *Herman Melville: A Study of His Life and Vision.* Rev. ed., New York: Harcourt, Brace and World, 1962.

Murray, Henry A. "In Nomine Diaboli," *NEQ,* 24 (December, 1951), 435–52.

Neider, Charles, ed. *Short Novels of the Masters.* New York: Rinehart, 1962.

Nilon, Charles Hampton. "Some Aspects of the Treatment of Negro Characters by Five American Novelists: Cooper, Melville, Tourgee, Glasgow, Faulkner." Doctoral dissertation, University of Wisconsin, 1952.

Pearce, Roy Harvey. "Melville's Indian-Hater: A Note on a Meaning of *The Confidence-Man.*" *PMLA,* 67 (December, 1952), 942–48.

Phillips, Barry. " 'The Good Captain': A Reading of *Benito Cereno.*" *Texas Studies in Literature and Language,* 4 (summer, 1962), 188–97.

Putzel, Max. "The Sources and the Symbols of Melville's *Benito Cereno.*" *American Literature,* 34 (May, 1962), 191–06.

Rosenberry, Edward H. "Melville's Ship of Fools." *PMLA,* 75 (December, 1960), 604–08.

Schiffman, Joseph. "Critical Problems in Melville's *Benito Cereno.*" *Modern Language Quarterly,* 11 (September, 1950), 317–24.

Sedgwick, William Ellery. *Herman Melville: The Tragedy of Mind.* Cambridge: Harvard University Press, 1944; rpt. New York: Russell and Russell, 1962.

Shroeder, John W. "Sources and Symbols for Melville's *Confidence-Man.*" *PMLA,* 66 (June, 1951), 363–80.

Stern, Milton R. *The Fine Hammered Steel of Herman Melville.* Urbana: University of Illinois Press, 1957.

Thompson, Lawrance. *Melville's Quarrel with God.* Princeton: Princeton University Press, 1952.

Thorp, Willard. Introduction to *Herman Melville: Representative Selections.* New York: American Book Company, 1938.

Vincent, Howard P. *The Trying-Out of Moby-Dick.* Carbondale: Southern Illinois University Press, 1965.

Watters, R. E. "Melville's 'Isolatoes.' " *PMLA,* 60 (December, 1945), 1138–48.

Weaver, Raymond. Introduction to *The Shorter Novels of Herman Melville.* New York: Fawcett Publications, 1964.